Teaching COLLEGE

Collected Readings for the New Instructor

Edited by Maryellen Weimer
and Rose Ann Neff

Atwood
Publishing
PO Box 3185
Madison, Wisconsin 53704

Sixth Printing

Printed in the United States of America

ISBN 1-891859-04-8 $21.95

Contents

Introduction

This collection contains ideas, information and advice for instructors teaching a college course for the first time. It is designed for teaching assistants, part-time instructors with no previous (or very little) college teaching experience, and faculty members assuming their first college teaching positions. This means the contents focus on the "essentials" of teaching, its bottom-lines, so to speak. These are the most obvious (and we would contend, important) issues that confront new teachers as they assume instructional responsibility for the first time.

We suspect that as a new instructor you will read this volume just before or during your first teaching experiences, a time when the day-by-day realities of preparing and conducting classes leave little room for reflective, thoughtful, scholarly reading — especially about teaching. This is why we found the idea of a collection of readings so appealing. The articles in this volume are short. They can be read over a sandwich, on the bus, or during those last few minutes before it's time to go home. They can also be read as they are needed, as the teaching experience itself raises the issues.

We organized the material in the volume semi-sequentially. We begin with some introductory issues and concerns, move to planning topics, then offer advice on instructional methods and finally address issues of evaluation. You might have time (and the desire) to read the whole volume before you start teaching. That's fine. If you are pushed for time, we suggest a cursory read-through, paying special attention to the section introductions which describe the intent and focus of each section. In other words, find out what's in the collection, and then you can go to the articles as they become relevant.

We're delighted that you have acquired this volume. There's so much to learn about teaching — and unfortunately too many of us who teach in college learned to teach by the seat of our pants in the school of hard knocks (if you'll permit the mixed metaphors). Sure, you can learn to teach that way, but it isn't always a pleasant process, nor is it the most efficient way of learning. You need to be encouraged to learn from the experience and mistakes of those of us who have preceded you and even a short book like this can do much to make your first experience in the classroom a good and positive one.

But it's much more than a case of your "elders" needing to "educate" their "juniors." Teaching (and learning how to teach) needs to be approached as a scholarly activity, something that demands intellectual attention and reflective analysis. This may be a new idea. If you've just finished graduate school or are in the middle of it, you aren't going to find a lot of attention devoted to teaching as a subject for scholarly study. Graduate education develops content-competency, mastery over the methods of a discipline. The prevalent assumption seems to be "if you know it, you can teach it."

Teaching, in fact, is a phenomenon in its own right. Certainly knowledge of the content helps to make it successful, but knowing the material is only part of being an effective instructor. Teachers do much more than simply transfer information to students. We inspire, serve as role models, function as leaders, establish and maintain standards, arbitrate conflicts — all complicated roles, demanding careful orchestration.

But you are taking a step in the right direction. Few of us who teach in college today confronted the task with a book in hand. We hope it will be the first of many you consult. You will not learn all you need to know about teaching by reading this book or any other. Teaching is far too complex to capture that concretely. Another mistake faculty (new and old) make is to assume that teaching can be reduced to a correct combination of techniques. What happens in class on any given day depends on a complex interplay of variables that we still only understand in the most rudimentary terms. You do need techniques, strategies, gimmicks, a whole bag of instructional tricks — but you must also learn *when* and *how* to use them.

Yes, you do have much to learn, but we can assure you, this will be some of the most exciting and personally enriching learning you'll ever do. Those of us committed to teaching excellence do tend to be idealists, on occasion effusive, but we speak the truth when we tell you that teachers have the power to change the way students think about themselves and their world. R.W. Packer says it more eloquently: "Probably the most violent and aggressive act that any person can do to other persons is to invade their minds with ideas and twists of meaning which disturb the comforting security of things known and faith kept. Yet this is what I, as a teacher, am required to do." (From "Breaking the Sound Barrier: A Dramatic Presentation" in *Teaching in the Universities: No One Way*.)

The Editors

SECTION 1

So You're Going to Teach a College Course

If your course starts next week and you just found out you'll be teaching it, you may want to skip this section now and move to the more immediate and practical concerns of Section 2. If you do that, do promise yourself to return. The issues, concerns and ideas raised by materials in this section need to be a part of college teachers' thinking from the beginning. We guarantee that you'll be addressing the issues we raise here before your first college teaching experience ends. We believe you'll respond more effectively if you start thinking about them now.

We start this section where we end the book: addressing evaluative issues. What makes good teaching? Does anybody know? How do you go about developing your skill as a teacher? Isn't the bottom line really the question of whether or not the students have learned the material? How much of that learning is your responsibility?

These questions don't have simple answers, but they do have answers. We know what makes teaching effective, from a solid empirical base. Moreover, the good news about those ingredients is that they are not divine gifts, but acquirable skills. But, as Hanna and McGill point, out good teaching involves much more than "stirring together a collection of appropriate ingredients." (p. 17) They encourage an emphasis on student learning as a sort of touchstone for teaching effectiveness. In addition to incorporating the ingredients of effective instruction, instructors are responsible for creating environments conducive to learning, places where students and teachers connect and move forward together in the quest for new knowledge.

So, new teachers need to start out thinking about the aims and purposes of education and how they will accomplish them. But those lofty and noble ideals must not separate new teachers from the instructional realities of the teaching-learning situation. Those of us who have been teaching for a number of years face a problem: we forget what it's like being a student. When you're new to the teaching role, maybe still young, it's easier to see things from the student's perspective. It's easier, but still not simple. You will be amazed how different the world looks from the front of the room. If you're like most of us, for the first time in your life you'll enjoy finals. To give is better than to receive. The euphoria wears off as you grade them, but it still feels pretty good.

The point, though, is that you never want to forget what it feels like to take a final. You must never forget the frustration that comes when you try with all your might to understand something — but find you can't. You must never forget how hard it is stay awake in a warm classroom at the end of a long week when only the professor finds the topic of interest. Starling makes the point even more dramatically: "There is a clear causal connection between these two statements: teachers get very little reliable feedback, and being a student really is 'a pain.'" (p. 21)

However, students today are not easy to teach. One of the most serious mistakes teachers make is to assume the students they have in class are the same kind of students they once were. If you're teaching a college course, in all probability you were an excellent student, and even if you didn't do all that handsomely in college, it was not because you lacked the intellectual ability. Most of the students you will have in class are not like you. You must be prepared for that and as you, like the rest of us, become astounded at their passivity, inadequate preparation, and lack of respect for learning, you will wonder about their irresponsibility. Unfortunately, part of the responsibility for the way they are belongs to us, which does mean we have the power to make changes. Coady illustrates: "We teach values when we refuse to tolerate procrastination, self-indulgence, laziness, or lack of any sense of priorities." (p. 28)

Despite their weaknesses, students today are still the wonderful creatures they have always been. They are still profoundly influenced by their experiences in college courses, particularly by their teachers. Research and our collected experience confirm that. They still glow with pride when they accomplish the unexpected and sometimes return to tell us we made a difference. Our success in dealing with them is inextricably linked to a clear understanding of their rights and our responsibilities. Their attitudes and abilities and those of our institutions that admit them make the boundaries between these distinctions fuzzy. It helps if new teachers are clear from the beginning as to who's responsible for what. Teaching does have important ethical dimensions.

And so, we recommend starting your college teaching career by thinking about these larger issues. Yes, the nuts and bolts demand more immediate attention, but the quality of life in your classroom depends to no small degree on the careful consideration of the concerns addressed in this section.

It's a Myth: Nobody Knows What Makes Teaching Good

Maryellen Weimer

Only anecdotal evidence supports this myth. "Believers" point to Dr. Dramatic down the hall who dances into and around the classroom. He's been known to play music, sing along, and one day he even cried in class. Students are spellbound, captivated, motivated. They say Dr. Dramatic is the best teacher they ever had. Believers then point down the other end of the hall and tell you about Dr. Dour. She is grim, believes the world may end before the semester does. The only possible way to avoid impending doom is to learn her drab, dusty content. She scolds students, mocks their naivete, and earns their respect. They say Dr. Dour is the best teacher they've ever had. So you see — decidedly different teaching styles are equally effective, and that proves it. Nobody knows what makes teaching good.

Wrong! Since the 1930s researchers have inquired as to the components of effective instruction. At this point, virtually everyone has been asked: students while they were in college, at graduation, and one, two, and 10 years after graduation; faculty from every discipline with a name (and maybe a few still unnamed); administrators from department heads to presidents. A variety of research methodologies have been used, including surveys and instructional observations. Collected research results have been organized, assessed, and otherwise subjected to meta-analysis. The problem is *not* that we do not know the answer to the question, What makes teaching good? The dilemma is that we have hundreds of answers.

Actually, it's not as bad as it may at first seem. Granted, every list of characteristics is different and nobody is in a position to say for sure which contains the right combination. But in general the answers aren't all that different. Some teacher characteristics keep turning up on list after list. Sherman et al. in the January/February 1987 issue of the *Journal of Higher Education* discuss five characteristics that have "consistently" been attributed to excellent instructors. These are:

- enthusiasm,
- clarity,
- preparation/organization,
- ability to stimulate, and
- knowledge (implying both content competence and love of the subject matter).

So, we do know (at least in some general sense) what makes teaching good. But the myth remains. And the fact that Doctors Dramatic and Dour teach differently is undeniable. What's the explanation?

The characteristics associated with good teaching are abstract. Their presence or absence in a given teaching performance must be inferred. The conclusion that an instructor is enthusiastic derives from certain behaviors like vocal variety, intense eye contact, gestures, and body movement. And this is where it does get complicated. Research has documented that there are many, many behaviors that convey enthusiasm. Doctor Dramatic does it by dancing around the room. Dr. Dour does it with direct, penetrating eye contact. Dr. Dour is not "enthusiastic" in the sense of being "lively," but the net result for both instructors is the same. They convince students that they care deeply about what they teach. The point, then, is that *the characteristics of good teaching are manifest in very different ways*. But there is still another complicating factor: We know what the characteristics are, but we don't know how they relate to each other. Do they interact synergistically? Can one component be missing and excellence in others compensate? At this point we have suppositions, not answers. However, if these components of good teaching can be present in different amounts (and some of us suspect this is so) with the net effect being recognized as effective instruction, then we have still another explanation for the variations of style among good teachers. More needs to be known about good teaching — but the assertion that nobody knows what makes teaching good is a myth.

It's a Myth: Good Teachers Are Born — Not Made

Maryellen Weimer

It's a companion myth to the one described in the preceding article, that nobody knows what makes teaching good. Remember Professors Dramatic and Dour, who teach in fundamentally different ways but with equal success? Well, adherents of this second myth (generally also believers in the first) would tell you that Dramatic and Dour were born teaching the way they do, and nothing much can be done about it. In this case, that's not a problem, since they both teach well.

But persons who believe good teachers are born have little encouragement to offer faculty who would like to improve. Quite simply, their advice is: "Don't try." Oh, they might admit to a few cosmetic alterations, but fundamentally, teaching is a God-given gift whose size is determined and fixed at birth. That's not a very optimistic view, and it calls into question a lot of other assumptions — like whether or not it's possible for students to learn beyond their natural gifts.

Fortunately, the belief that good teachers are born is a myth and can be dispelled by two arguments. Some may discredit the first because it's more experiential than empirical — but if something happened to you, you don't argue with it. Most of us with any years at all behind the lectern know that the way we teach has changed. Some of us grimace when we recollect our first feeble attempts to dispense knowledge. The school of hard knocks isn't the most pleasant place in which to learn, but learn we did. In some cases, we can document the change with gradually improving student evaluations. In other cases, it is a deep, abiding conviction that we're doing better than we used to. So — teaching performance does change. And we know it experientially from the other direction too. We've seen or heard of colleagues who've drifted away from teaching — whose once-lively classrooms are now still and deadly.

The second argument is more likely to convince the doubters. We prove to them that the components of effective instruction are acquirable. To do that we harken back to the first myth and a point made in the preceding article. We do know from a strong empirical base what the components of good teaching are — things like enthusiasm, preparation, organization, clarity, among others. The research results are not surprising. They tell us pretty much what we expected. The secrets to success in the classroom are not mysterious, but ordinary things, like being enthusiastic, organized and clear. That's the good news.

The bad news is that acquiring these skills is not as easy as it might first appear. *You do not become enthusiastic by deciding what you will be tomorrow in class.* You may pull it off tomorrow, but in terms of sustained behavior change, this sort of global assault is not generally successful — which partly accounts for the continuing popularity of the myth that teachers are born, not made.

Some of the difficulty derives from the fact that characteristics of good teaching are highly abstract. They are not concrete entities that one goes out and acquires. However, the characteristics manifest themselves as behaviors. Enthusiastic instructors *do* certain things that convey their interest and energy. We can identify what those behaviors are: they move about, gesture, let their faces show emotion, look intently at students, and vary their tone of voice, for example.

Now the argument against the myth gains momentum. The behaviors that communicate enthusiasm, as well as the other components of good instruction, are not things that only a gifted few can do. Most faculty members are able to walk around more during lectures, most could on occasion move their arms, and the majority can change the intensity of their eye contact.The actual process of making instructional changes works this way. To begin, the teacher must have a clear sense of instructional self. Armed with a knowledge of what one actually *does* when he's teaching, one can look for behaviors that convey known aspects of good teaching, like enthusiasm for example. The key to success then becomes selecting appropriate behaviors, given the proclivities of style of the instructor involved.

If, for example, the professor routinely presents material with lectern firmly in hand, then conveying enthusiasm through vigorous strides across the front of the room is probably not a good suggestion — but looking more directly at students may be. So, the instructor ends up incorporating into her teaching style behaviors that are associated with good teaching and behaviors that, given certain caveats, come naturally.

The myth is dispelled — almost. The components of good teaching are known and can be transformed into acquirable skills. Good teachers are not just born: they can be made. However,

15

there is a magic about truly effective instruction that defies description. By comparison, an improvement process like this smacks of being mechanical, and teaching at its best is never studied or contrived. It happens naturally, spontaneously, and with tremendous power. Kenneth Eble may have the answer. In his fine book, *The Craft of Teaching*, he writes:

> The more I have looked at teachers, the more I come back to an old truth of human existence: We are both born and made. At most, some teachers may have certain natural advantages: high intelligence, verbal fluency, patience, a capacity for service, good looks, a pleasant speaking voice, charm, a mind for detail, a good memory, a head for generalizations. Most of these skills are as likely to be acquired as inborn, and, when examined closely, all lose the aura of mysterious capabilities that some people have and others haven't or that some can develop and others can't. (pp. 17-18)

A Nurturing Environment and Effective Teaching

Stanley J. Hanna and Lawrence T. McGill

It is difficult to state exactly what constitutes effective teaching. Many lists of "criteria" have been suggested, ranging from character traits to teaching styles to alternative interaction strategies, as if an effective teacher could be produced by stirring together a collection of appropriate ingredients. We encourage a more holistic approach to this issue, as well as an emphasis upon student learning components of teaching effectiveness. By paying attention in particular to the affective aspects of learning, we hope to suggest a more useful conception of the idea of teaching effectiveness and how it may be assessed.

The primary purpose of evaluating teacher effectiveness is to improve education. By identifying what constitutes effective teaching, we can strive toward this goal. Typically, this task requires that we analyze and evaluate teachers to find out who are the most effective ones, what traits or style they use, who are the less effective ones, and how we may improve their skills. This task also requires that we determine what sorts of criteria might be used for evaluating teacher effectiveness, as Ostrowski points out:

> The ultimate purpose for evaluating teachers is to enhance student achievement.
> However, student gain as a single criterion is not sufficient to judge effective
> teaching. Multiple criteria should be simultaneously assessed that have a definite
> part in deciding who is effective.

Problems in establishing acceptable criteria for evaluating teachers arise because the criteria must adequately cover the social roles as well as give fair value to the teacher's personal attributes and manner. Also, the criteria must cover the functional or managerial role, account for individual differences of teachers and students, and be measurable and observable within a reasonable length of time.

Crist and Achilles (1980) argue that only through a holistic approach can we discover "what is good teaching" and not impose a definition of "what it may be." They believe that superior teaching "may emerge from large numbers of variables interacting, not from a limited few which have been isolated to make them easier to observe." (p. 27) By examining effective teaching as isolated bits of behavior, we imply that some data about it are more valuable than are other data. By presuming to know which bits constitute effectiveness, we miss the many affective characteristics which combine as integral parts of a holistic model for effective teaching. We must be "less concerned with what is planned and designed and more intent on that which occurs without intrusion ... sensitive to the unique, spontaneous, and unexpected." (p. 27)

Experience suggests that affective components of learning are of critical import if students are to make measurable gains in acquiring and manipulating knowledge. Aspy and Roebuck (1974) hypothesized and subsequently verified that "people who received high levels of Empathy, Congruence, and Positive Regard would attain more growth than those who had been given low levels of them." (p. 164) The teacher who provides high levels of these three conditions enhances students' growth. The teacher who does not inhibits student learning.

Prerequisites of Teaching Effectiveness

Four sets of competencies, described in various ways by researchers, seem to stand out when teachers, identified as excellent at the community college level, describe how they behave in various situations. Most lists of criteria for effective teaching are derived, in fact, from these sets of competencies. According to Baker, Boggs, and Putnam (1983), these effective teachers displayed:

- a student-centered orientation
- a value for the learning process
- a need to influence individual behavior, and
- a belief that they possessed the power to produce a desired effect in the learner.

These four may not be all-inclusive, but they are the basis for the ideal environment in which to nurture excellence — in both student and teacher. "It is the combined efforts of effective teachers and administrators that establishes an institutional environment conducive to excellence in teaching and learning." (p. 29)

Klemp, Schneider, and Kastendick (1982) touch upon these same attributes of effective teachers in their discussion of mentoring. They describe it as "The Balancing Act." The heart of the effective teachers' balancing act, they observed, was the ability to balance student-centeredness with firm direction.

Like Baker, Boggs, and Putnam, they concluded that those teachers considered to be particularly effective in classroom teaching and one-to-one mentoring were student-centered. The characteristic which distinguished the effective teachers from those considered to be average was their optimism about, and affirmation of, the accomplishments of average and even exceptionally difficult students. Their positive expectations, reflecting both their desire and belief that they can influence students, was a notably powerful theme in interviews with effective teachers. The average teachers' expression of negative expectations was their single most dominant theme. The average teachers lacked awareness of, and responsiveness to, particular student concerns and needs. The effective teachers were more likely to remember the details of their interactions with students and to know what the outcomes of a particular situation with a student had been.

The message being sent by Klemp et al. is that students need to know that we believe fully in them; that we believe they can succeed; and that we do care about them and their uniqueness. As child development specialists have pointed out, caring need not always be associated with permissiveness.

> When conflicts arose between the students' external concerns and the demands of their learning, the effective teachers held their students accountable. They were persuasive and, when necessary, firm or confrontive when student concerns threatened to interfere with learning (Klemp, Schneider, and Kastendick, 1983).

Firm directiveness and truly high expectations of students often is translated by students into a belief that effective teachers sincerely care about learning, about them, and, as their mentor, about their success.

Klemp et al. also found effective teachers to be characterized by a pervasive conviction that learning is a highly valuable activity. These teachers presented themselves as learners, aligning themselves with their students in a common cause — learning. The average teachers, while often espousing an appreciation for humanistic education, never described themselves as directly engaged in learning. They taught in ways that implied their greater commitment to exposing students to subject and discipline approaches.

The effective teachers placed great emphasis on making use of their students' interests, attitudes, and experiences in the learning process. They created learning situations in which it was the student who worked through the course issues, questions, or exercises and arrived at an understanding of the learning points in question.

Attributes of Effective Learners

Often, attempts to define what we mean by effective teaching tend to overlook the most important issue, which is what constitutes student learning. A concurrent issue, therefore, is whether or not the attributes of the effective teacher imply reciprocal attributes among effective learners. That is:

- Are effective learners self-centered with respect to learning, thus allowing the student-centered orientation of the effective teacher to pay off via the student's self-growth?

- Do effective learners share with effective teachers a value for the learning process?

- Do they feel a need to be influenced by the teacher insofar as pertinent outcomes to the learning process are concerned?

- Do effective learners believe in the ability of the teacher to produce a desired effect in the learner?

Clearly, the negation of each of these attributes would constitute hindrances to learning. A student who is not self-centered, but say teacher- or grade-centered for example, will ultimately behave in such a fashion as to either minimize expressions of negative regard from the teacher or to achieve high marks on exams. Certainly, each of these also tend to follow from true mastery of the subject matter, but as many a disillusioned college student can attest, material can be learned in such a way as to pass exams or please instructors without so much as making a mark upon the intellectual development of the student. Among undergraduates, an ethos of instrumentalism prevails, which subverts intentions to internalize the subject matter, channeling efforts to compile a better-looking transcript than that of fellow students (Becker, 1968). Such an environment tends to foster a general disregard for the value of learning for learning's sake, thus negating the second attribute of effective learners as well as the first.

With regard to the third, we need only ask if it is conceivable that a teacher could be effective in an environment in which students feel no need to consider the teacher to be a potential source of influence upon them. Finally, it is also clear that students who have no faith in the ability of a teacher to effect intellectual changes in them have effectively closed their minds to the possibility of in-class learning.

Identification and Exemplification

The point is that teachers can be effective only to the extent that the learner allows them to be. Given this, what can teachers do to help students along toward the attitudes needed to be effective learners?

Two concepts — the processes of "identification" and "exemplification" — seem central. In some sense, what marks an effective teacher is an ability to convince students that the teacher is on their side; that what the students want is also what the teacher wants. This process can be referred to as "identification," in the sense that identification means the taking of something external to the self into one's own identity. To the extent that we get students saying to themselves, "I can identify with that" as we interact with them, we succeed on each of the four dimensions of teaching effectiveness from both the teacher's and the learner's points of view.

As important as it is for students to achieve a sense of identification with what's being taught, teachers also have an equivalent obligation to develop a sense of identification with students. Klemp, Schneider, and Kastendick (1983) describe part of what this entails:

> Characteristically, effective teachers begin the process of identifying learning tasks
> by actively unearthing information about their students' learning needs and
> interests. But information seeking [is] only the beginning of a larger process.
> [Effective teachers] also exhibited skills in integrating disparate information about
> their students into diagnostic theories that, in turn, yielded prescriptions for action
> that would further their students' learning.

Effective teachers, in other words, look to their students (as well as into themselves) for clues as to what steps need to be taken to improve students' understanding of subject matter.

The other concept which seems to typify effective teaching is that of "exemplification." While the effective teacher must cast one eye toward the needs and goals of students, the other eye must be directed toward the subject matter. Effective teachers are not only imparting information to students, but are also revealing their particular ways of acquiring, understanding, and making use of that information.

The concept of exemplification is derived from the four characteristics of the effective learner. Most specifically, it derives from the claim that just as the effective teacher feels a need to influence students, the effective learner feels a need to be influenced by a teacher. The aphorism that people learn best when they learn by example is another way of stating this principle. Students look to teachers not only as sources of information, but as role models also.

What the juxtaposition of these two concepts should also point out is the difficulty and complexity of being an effective teacher. Not only does that person strive to achieve a sense of identification between student and teacher, but he or she must also exemplify an appropriate way of investigating one's subject matter. After all, what the effective teacher ultimately wants the student to identify with is an exemplary way of doing work in one's field.

Using Affect to Good Effect

The issue then may be how to incorporate using these characteristics into teaching methodology. Irwin Sayer (1972) concluded that "no clear patterns have emerged which favour any specific methods of instruction" at the college level in order to improve achievement. However, as Klemp,

Schneider, and Kastendick (1983) described above, the affective environmental issues are of primary importance to effective teaching at this level. Thus, Sayer's results make sense.

It is not the *method*, within reason, which determines effective teaching and student success, but the *affective environment* created that nurtures success from whatever method the teacher feels most comfortable using. Certainly apparent success results from environments which reflect the characteristics of negativism and fear. One wonders what kind of learning takes place, how long it lasts, and what student types do not succeed, not because of personal failure, but because of the environment.

Donald Medley points out that:

> One largely unanswered question about the nature of teacher effectiveness is whether a teacher who is effective in producing one kind of gains with one kind of pupil may also be expected to be equally effective in producing other kinds of gains with other kinds of pupils. Is teacher effectiveness general or specific to the kind of pupil taught and the kind of outcome measured?

This is a legitimate area of concern. When we understand that affective characteristics constitute a significant source of influence on student success, then we can answer Medley's question: teaching effectiveness can be generalized when a nurturing environment has been established.

References

Aspy, David, & Roebuck, Flora. "From Human Ideas to Human Technology and Back Again Many Times." *Education*, Winter 1974.

Baker, George; Boggs, George; & Putnam, Scottie. "Ideal Environment Nurtures Excellence." *Community and Junior College Journal*, October 1983.

Becker, Howard; Greer, Blanche; & Hughes, Everette. *Making the Grade.* New York: John Wiley, 1968.

Crist, Michael, & Achilles, C.M. "The Assessment of College Teaching." *National Forum*, Spring 1980.

Klemp, George; Schneider, Carol; & Kastendick, Susan. *The Balancing Act: Competencies of Effective Teachers and Mentors.* Chicago: University of Chicago, Office of Continuing Education, 1982.

Medley, Donald. "Research In Teacher Effectiveness — Where It Is and How It Got There." Manuscript for book to be published by The National Society for the Study of Education.

Ostrowski, Michael V. *A Comparison of Grades Students Achieved at William Rainey Harper College (Ill.) and How They Rate the Effectiveness of Their Instructor of Midterm, During the Spring of 1975 Semester.* ERIC File ED 110113.

Sayer, Irwin; Campbell, James Reed; & Barns, Cyrus. "The Effect of College Instructors' Interaction Ratios on Cognitive Development." *Science Education*, 56:4 (1972).

Professor as Student: The View From the Other Side

Roy Starling

"Nobody knew how to be what they were right." [1]

If you ever have the opportunity, as I did, to become an undergraduate again, don't expect it to be much fun. One evening when a colleague saw me at the computer, writing yet another paper, he said, "Every time I see you up here, I'm reminded of what a pain in the butt it is to be a student." And it is. Giving up the power of a teacher for the vulnerability of a student is not a good trade. But the real pain came when I saw how often I had made a mess of the profession I loved, had done badly the thing I do best.

It is difficult for us to know how effective we are as teachers. Here at Rollins College, we get most of our feedback from student evaluations, filled out anonymously at the end of each term. By this time, the students, if they like the teacher, figure the damage has been done and the term is over with, so why worry about it now? Or they may feel that since they are only students, who are they to tell the teacher how to do his or her job? Then, of course, there is the revenge evaluation, where the student simply attempts to get back (usually in large print with plenty of exclamation points) at the teacher for some earlier injustice, real or imagined.

Community of Learners

With such little and such unreliable feedback, it may be tempting for us to combine two cliches — "Ignorance is bliss" and "If it ain't broke, don't fix it" — and grind our way down the road toward retirement. But at Rollins, since the formation of the Community of Learners program,[2] this route may eventually become the road not taken. Each term, a different faculty member is released from all teaching duties and becomes an undergraduate, taking a full course load with a group of 12 to 15 students.

This program, adapted from Professor Patrick Hill's Federated Learning Communities at SUNY-Stony Brook, was designed primarily to introduce freshmen and sophomores to the concept of collaborative learning and to give them the opportunity to study with a professor (called the master-learner) as a classmate. But those of us who have reprised our roles as students are more impressed with the unique perspective it gives teachers of their profession: I can think of no better way to gain a re-vision of teaching.

Going into the program, Barbara Carson (Rollins' first master-learner) was already generally considered one of the most effective teachers on campus. But after her term as a master-learner, she made some drastic changes. She used fewer lectures and more discussions, relied more heavily on journals than examinations, rearranged her office furniture to create a warmer and more open atmosphere, and changed from Dr. Carson to Barbara, and sometimes even Barb.

The master-learner experience forced me to acknowledge that there is a clear causal connection between these two statements: a) teachers get very little reliable feedback, and b) being a student really is "a pain." On certain days, I couldn't wait to return to teaching to put my new-found knowledge to work; on other days, the prospect of trying to fix so much that was broken led me to consider less demanding professions. Finally, I came around to the philosophy reflected in St. Francis' prayer: "God grant me the serenity to accept the things I cannot change, courage to change the things I can, and wisdom always to tell the difference." As a student I immediately became more aware of the imperfections of the system ("the things I cannot change") most of us must now work within. And, in fact, about all we can do about these imperfections is to be aware of them, to remember them.

Chief among these is that we rush students, feverishly, through the art gallery of education. At the beginning of the term, we fire the starting gun, telling them that in 14 weeks (at Rollins) they will have had rewarding learning experiences in four, sometimes five, classes. In the course of a term, we know that they will be exposed to numerous new ideas, and we expect them to integrate many of these; they will take in volumes of new information, and we expect them to store much of it ("What? You're an English major and you don't know what synecdoche is? What are they teaching you over there?").

This was one of the first lessons I learned (and I kept learning it and relearning it throughout the term) as a master-learner: the students aren't really "ours"; they are merely working us into a cluttered, hectic academic and social schedule. The experience of the first week of classes demonstrates clearly the false echo that students sound throughout their academic careers: the professor's "You will learn" answered by the student's "I will survive."

In the first week as a student, I went to my first class, was told the requirements for that course, and was warned that it wouldn't be easy. In the second class, we did some group work (about which I will say more later) and went over the course requirements. We had to walk through rain to get to the third class and found the room's air-conditioner set at somewhere near the igloo level. Wet, cold, tired, and with enough (we thought) to do already, we listened to another set of requirements: daily assignments, short papers, a long paper, seven novels, and a good share of reading on reserve at the library. Like the weary mariners of Tennyson's "Lotos-Eaters" (and remember, this was only two days into the term), I wanted to tell the professor, "Let us alone!"

But as professors we are competing with three or four other classes for the attention of our students. If we don't want them to put our class on the bottom of their list, we have to give them plenty of work. And when students are given plenty of work by all their professors, college mimics the military boot camp while still purporting to be a setting for meaningful learning. I found, as master-learners before me had found, that there were times when the workload was so heavy that it was impossible to complete in the time allotted, much less complete it with energy and imagination.

On such occasions, I observed students taking one of two courses of action: they ingested large quantities of caffeine (by way of either coffee or diet pills), pulled all-nighters, finished most of the work, and damaged their health; or, having inventoried the workload, they despaired of finishing it, didn't do any of it (a sin of omission popularly known as "blowing it off"), got drunk with other despairing students, and damaged their health.

To mitigate the boot camp syndrome when I return to teaching, I will do the following:

- Borrowing from one of my former professors, I will design group work for the first day of classes that will introduce students both to each other and to the subject matter. This sort of exercise gives everyone a chance to talk on the first day (and if some students don't speak out quite early in the term, they won't speak out at all) and, since it exposes the students to the course's intellectual content, they are more likely to leave this first class pondering ideas than dreading assignments.

- I will tell my students the rationale behind their assignments: "What I hope you will gain from this assignment is ...." "When reading Frye's essay, look especially for ...." "Writing a paper such as this will give you an opportunity to ...." Without such explanatory statements, students often feel they are being given busy-work. When they feel this way, they often spend more energy telling their friends what the professor can do with such assignments than working on the assignments.

- I will assign no superfluous material. I will be honest enough to admit that, given the restrictions of a 14-week course and a four-course term, it is not necessary to give equal attention to every word of a 700-page novel: "In this course, we will focus chiefly on ...." I will not suggest that my students trade in their texts for Cliff's Notes, but rather try to lessen the need for such shortcuts by engaging in some appropriate creative corner-cutting myself.

- Knowing now that student gripes are often legitimate, I will complain less about complaining students. Before my master-learner experience, I worried that students didn't take their school work seriously enough; now, I worry that many of them take it too seriously. I will now be more sympathetic, more flexible, preferring to be taken in by several students than to push one over the edge.

In short, I will try for the "serenity to accept that which I cannot change."

Rituals That Need Scrutiny

My experience taught me, however, that our system contains some dusty relics that can be changed, if we have the courage to do so. The first of these is the in-class, blue-book exam, a tradition so old that I am a little afraid to challenge its effectiveness. Many of us regard this ancient device as a rite of passage ("since I had to take them, you're going to have to take them"); worse yet, we seem to consider its presence as inevitable as a family curse or a hereditary disease. Before my master-learner experience, for example, I gave in-class, blue-book exams that closely resembled the ones my favorite professor gave me. (Interestingly, I gave the kind of exam that I always used to do well with as a younger student, thus rewarding those who shared my learning style and "nailing" those who did not.)

I now think that this type of exam hampers the learning process at two critical stages: during the integration of ideas (i.e., the preparation for the exam) and during the expression of the now (supposedly) integrated ideas (i.e., the actual taking of the exam). As a master-learner, while preparing for one exam, I studied both by myself and with the group, and in neither case was the emphasis on becoming a better-informed or wiser human being.

The text on which we were being tested (Eric Chaisson's *Cosmic Dawn*, a concise history of the universe) addressed the fundamental questions of life: Where did we come from? How did life begin? How do we survive the Atomic Age? But the questions that arose during study sessions were "Do you really think he'll ask us that?" "Do you think we actually need to know the number of stars in an elliptical galaxy?" "Will this be short answer or essay?" "Hey, has anyone had this guy before?" As master-learner, I was not too successful at refocusing their questions because I was afraid that, under the circumstances, their focus might have been about right.

In short, the threat of an upcoming exam, while encouraging students to become better acquainted with new ideas, may at the same time create too much tension to allow the desired integration of these ideas to take place. Admittedly, the anxiety-induced adrenalin gave our group the energy for some lively study sessions, and some of us even felt we had studied too much.[3] But my fellow students and I seemed to be holding the material in front of our minds just long enough to deposit it in the blue books; we saw no need to integrate something that we must soon "give back on an exam." The conventional exam, then, encouraged us to rent, not buy, new ideas.[4]

"Giving back" material on exam day, of course, poses problems of its own. Granted, there are a handful of students who are capable of doing what we want them to during this process: they read the instructions carefully, then analyze the question to be sure they know exactly what we're looking for, take a few minutes to map out their pattern of organization, then write, quickly, demonstrating how well they have understood the material, having, in fact, some new insights in the very act of writing, until, with five minutes remaining, they go back over the essay and check for omissions and mechanical blunders.

But consider the obstacles students face in this situation. They must quickly come to terms with an exam question that they may not have anticipated and/or one that is poorly or ambiguously worded. (Our questions always make perfectly good sense to us, but perhaps we should run them by a colleague or even by the campus writing center just to be sure we are communicating clearly.) Students who are subject to writing blocks must then find a way to get started. Some can't. During our first exam, for example, the intensely intelligent student sitting next to me stared at his blue book for about an hour, finally wrote a sentence, thought better of it, erased it, put his name on the front, and turned it in. (The erased sentence, still slightly visible, was so profound that the professor gave him points for it.)

If the block is conquered, the clock immediately becomes the enemy. The writing process — normally a thoughtful, laborious, time-consuming task — is crunched into an unnaturally rushed, often incoherent frenzy, into fast-forward, first-draft race-writing. There is no time for the student to dress up his new ideas in the clothes they deserve; in the tension of the moment, even integrated ideas refuse to come at the student's bidding, though some will stick their heads out just far enough to be decapitated in the transcribing process. Regardless of what the well-intentioned question asked for and regardless of the professor's admonition to "organize your essay well," the student believes (knows?), especially in the final minutes, that the most critical task is to relay as much information as possible in the limited time available. Often, then, we reward the student with the best small-motor muscles, the ones who can write the fastest. For the most part, exam-takers are racing, not learning.

Not that the conventional exam is a worthless endeavor. It does help students practice strategic thinking as they attempt to guess the enemy's (i.e., the professor's) secret plans for that dark hour. Exams also give students a chance to become accustomed to the anxiety, fear, and dread that will invariably accompany the stressful situations they will encounter down the road, in the game of life — that great series of exams. But if we are more interested in learning how well they are understanding the material in our course and in giving them a fair opportunity to share that understanding with us, I think there is a better way.

Near the end of the term, Dr. Karl Peters, the professor in our class, "Creation in Science and Religion," happened upon a poem in which he saw elements of the entire course. About four days before our final, he gave us a copy of this poem and asked us to "creatively analyze" it in light of all we had discussed during the course; he encouraged us to work on it as a group, and he allowed us to bring notes and texts (but no drafts) to class on exam day.

Consequently, all of the guesswork and much of the anxiety were immediately eliminated. We were free to review the course material, to synthesize it, to make sense of a term's work, and then to apply our new knowledge to fresh material, the poem. The group study session for this exam was, not surprisingly, a vast improvement over our earlier efforts. We went right to the heart of the matter, sharing our widely varied ideas on the poem and our occasionally differing memories of the course's important issues. No one stayed up late, worrying or studying, the night before the exam; almost everyone wrote constantly for the two hours allotted — no blocking or early surrenders.

Paper-Writing Process

My experience as a master-learner also forced me to re-examine the traditional method of assigning papers; while I found that I learned more while writing papers than I did preparing for and taking exams, I also noticed some potential problems with papers. The familiar method of putting a request for a paper or papers on the syllabus, keeping mum about them until the due date, taking them up, putting a grade on them in ink, and giving them back to the student — this method severely limits many students' ability to perform well.

Whenever we fail to maintain a continuing dialogue with students, the following tends to happen: many of them will worry about where to put their names, page numbers, that sort of thing; since some of their teachers care nothing about matters of format and others have a Platonic image of The Format, the students' worry is justified. If students receive no feedback from the professor once the paper is in process, they will usually settle for writing about what they already know, perhaps on a safe topic that is considered universally acceptable. This cautious piece of drivel results in little if any learning and will earn from the bored professor an autopsy such as the following: "Dave, this is basically error-free writing, but your thesis is not a very interesting one. Your paper contains little original thought. Be consistent with your footnoting! C+."

There is no reason to nip the learning process so severely in the bud. Learning can and will take place in the paper-writing process if the professor will:

- Remove the students' fear of or preoccupation with clerical matters by telling them which of these seemingly trivial trappings are actually of importance.

- Be honest about "what we want" in the paper. We naturally want students to take some initiative, to use their imagination, and to put their own special mark on the paper. But I know from experience — quite recent experience — that using one's imagination can be a risky proposition, that the student's special mark may not correspond with what the professor wants.

When we asked one of our professors what he wanted in a particular paper, he responded, as I often have: "Don't ask me that." I tried and failed in three separate drafts to find an appropriate angle on the general topic of alienation. When I was almost ready to give up and resort to a kind of book report, it came to me (and at the time, I called it inspiration) that I should take a semiautobiographical approach while allowing the theme to be reflected in the organization.

As is often the case, the end result of the writing process surprised me; it surprised my professor, too, but not pleasantly. His comments left little doubt that my personal approach was not what he wanted. Now I know what my students have been saying all these years when they see my end comments: "Oh, so he does know what he wants; he just won't say so until it's too late." We do have preconceived notions of "good" and "bad" essays, and after years of teaching, these notions may begin to harden, perhaps becoming carved in stone so that our grading of papers is made easier by our merely holding a student's paper up next to the granite one in our heads. And if it is a bad match, which essay will be termed "good"?

Finally, we should be sure that students have the opportunity to receive intelligent feedback throughout the writing process. They need to know if they're on the right track, if they're making any sense, if there is room for improvement. Like us, students need feedback every time they make a breakthrough and every time the paper takes a slightly different turn. Specialists in contemporary rhetoric have compared writing a paper to having a baby; I am merely asking that we wait until the baby is born before slapping a grade on it.

As a master-learner I learned that some things never change: the term paper, for instance, is still seldom a paper that is worked on for most of the term. Rather, it is still a heavy, sprawling monster that students take great delight in slaying the night before it is due. And I remembered why. Students generally have a little something to do for each meeting of each of their four classes. Even the good ones often fall behind in these assignments. On those rare occasions when everything is taken care of, nothing else to do before bedtime, nothing to dread for tomorrow, how many of us would feel like beginning a lengthy research paper?

As the oldest member of the group, I provided a positive role model by selecting a topic in the second week of class and checking out a few books so I could begin my research in my spare time. As the course progressed, however, my topic no longer seemed appropriate and my spare time disappeared altogether. Ultimately, I wrote the paper over a three-day period; about the best I could do was a slightly cleaned-up first draft. Some of my fellow students completed theirs in two days, while others maintained the tradition of the one-night paper.

To sabotage the students' attempts to write their term papers during the course of an evening, I plan to assign not one, but three due dates. After the first one, about a month into the term, I can comment on the paper's topic; when the paper is resubmitted a month later, I can give advice concerning organization and bibliography. The final draft, then, will have had the benefit of a little more time and a little more direction than the traditional one-nighter.

The fact that I salvaged the term paper while attempting to make it a more valuable learning tool indicates that my master-learner experience made me neither an anarchist nor a revolutionary, nor did it return me to the dreamy idealism of my first year of teaching. I am not a child rejecting the wisdom of the preceding generation; rather, I have learned that, if we want to make college safe for learning, the "rituals" of our profession must be carefully scrutinized with each passing term. Such scrutiny is the only way that we will gain the wisdom to tell the difference between the things we can change and the things we cannot.

EXAM!

Before ...

Three days before the exam. No more role-playing now, no more pretending to be a worried student — I *am* one. The pre-exam tension headache and nervous stomach of yesteryear show up like unexpected in-laws. I try to ease out of the role and make the exam not matter. I am a grown-up, a colleague of the man who's doing this to me, a professor simply participating in this program my college has cooked up, going along with their little game for a while.

Doesn't help, the exam still matters. I study too late, then dream that exam day is here and I haven't studied at all. I dream the exam is actually in sociology, and I've been studying religion. The night before the exam, I close the books early and watch a Celtics game I've taped just for this depressurization. It works. The Celtics win and I sleep soundly.

Exam morning — what a mixture of energy, excitement, anxiety, and fear. No one sits while waiting to get in the classroom. All stand, some jump. Plenty of silly jokes, many of them treating irreverently the material we've been studying. We go in. The professor arrives. No one is glad to see this man we all like and no one wants to see him smile because now we see it as a demonic grin. He knows what he's going to ask and what we're supposed to say. And now the ritualistic distributing of the blue books, *empty* blue books.

During ...

And now he distributes the exams and maybe the worst time of all arrives: reading the essay question — so cleverly, so cunningly devised by him. (I know how he did it. Late at night, leaning over the computer, grinning and rubbing his hands together with delight.) Reading it word by word, dreading the next word, the one that may permanently block the flow of ink from my pen, the one that steals my angle, robbing me of the tidy essay my brain has been so carefully constructing for the past week, the one word that asks me to explain the one part of the book I never quite grasped ... ah! not this time. But wait a second. How will I get all I know on paper in only an hour? What do I omit? Exactly how fast can I write?

STARTǃ I begin the awful fast-forward writing, most of it desperate, some of it almost saying, "Please, you know what I mean." On a crucial point, my memory goes fuzzy — how do I touch on the subject (I can't omit it) without revealing the fuzziness? Hand aches, neck stiffens. Get to the point, get to the point. But I have to lead up to it with details to demonstrate my knowledge of the material, and if I make my point too soon, what will I finish the exam with? Will I go back and add things in the margins?

Fifteen minutes to go, not enough time to reach the punch line with any grace or subtlety, let alone re-read what I've done. Skip planet formation, go directly to the development of the brain. But how to do that? "Now, skipping over the formation of planets ...⁇? If only I had a few more minutes, but time's up.

After ...

Over. Done. That's it. I did OK. I studied enough, gave it my best shot. Drained. Used up. Need to talk to classmates. Think about it. I didn't even discuss one of the most important terms. I omitted several critical dates. B+? I *should* have said. I *shouldn't* have said. Don't think about it.

Notes

[1] John Barth, "Lost in the Funhouse." From *Lost in the Funhouse* (New York: Bantam, 1968), p. 81.

[2] The Community of Learners' three-year existence at Rollins has been made possible by a grant from Harcourt Brace Jovanovich, Inc.

[3] For whatever reason, our next exam evoked a completely opposite effect: we could hardly force ourselves to read the material, and when we held a study session, it quickly deteriorated into a giddy giggle session. We left comfortable in the knowledge that we would all do poorly on the exam the next day, and so none of us would look that bad. How were we to know that one of our group would go home and study for three hours, then completely destroy the curve (and the rest of us) on the exam?

[4] I made an A on the exam, but now, just a few months later, I have forgotten the temperature required for nuclear burning, and I confess that I had to look up "elliptical galaxy," mentioned above, to be sure there is such a thing.

Student Irresponsibility: We Helped Cause It

Sharon Coady

Dave says he can't take the test today — when can he make it up? Susan wants to go to Florida next week — she'll get notes on what she'll miss from a friend when she gets back. Angie didn't get a chance to study last night — may she take the quiz tomorrow instead of today? Bob didn't do too well on the test — when can he take it over?

Student irresponsibility is a problem teachers have always complained about, but it seems to me it has grown remarkably worse during the past few years. In fact, irresponsible behavior seems to have increased in all parts of society as self-discipline and responsibility have lost power as social values. Nevertheless, I think that we in education have helped cause our own problem.

We have focused so intently on teaching that we have relieved the student of the responsibility for learning. With the flurry of experiments in the 1960s and the mania for objectives in the 1970s we abandoned the teaching of such values as responsibility and embraced objectives that could be reduced to the simplest, most measurable terms. In the pursuit of clarity, fairness, and definition, we have transmitted some unintended messages.

Mastery learning. Goals and objectives. Student-oriented learning objectives. Behavioral objectives. We as teachers know what they all mean, and what good effects they should produce. But what do they say, indirectly, to the students?

- Failure is never your fault. It's due to bad teaching.

- You can make up anything. If at first you don't succeed — if at first you don't *try* to succeed — take the test again, and again, and again. There is always a second chance.

- There's no penalty for fouling up. There's another quiz where that one came from; there may be more financial aid for another semester.

- You're not responsible for your actions. We know you have children and you have to work and you're carrying 18 credits. We understand. Life is tough. You may have a week's extension on the paper.

The difficulty is that the basic philosophy of education is good. It sees students as whole people who have dimensions to their lives outside the classroom. It recognizes that not everyone can succeed the first time around or learn in exactly 15 weeks. It has forced teachers to examine what they do and make some badly needed changes.

Mastery learning makes sense. You measure what people know rather than the hours they sit in lecture hall seats.

Goals and clearly stated objectives not only benefit students; they force teachers to define precisely what they want to accomplish and to make a rational link between what they say they want to do and what they in fact are doing.

I can even find a few good words to say about behavioral objectives. When used properly they can help a floundering student and also clarify the teacher's thinking.

Student-oriented learning objectives can relieve students' anxieties and tell them exactly what they must learn.

Despite the good intentions, those methods can also encourage irresponsibility and a lack of self-discipline among students. Students for the most part do not have to train themselves to produce on demand, think quickly, work efficiently, or deny today's pleasure in favor of a greater payoff tomorrow. Their skills are weakened and their learning lessened because they take so little responsibility for learning.

When I was in college, a professor of European history seared his image — and a lot of European history — on my memory by placing all responsibility for what I learned on my shoulders. A hundred of us filed into the lecture hall on the first day. After the initial formalities, he handed us a six-page, single-spaced bibliography. "Read what you think you ought to know to pass the course," he said.

It may have been an extreme measure, but for me and most of the others in that class it worked. We learned.

The new methods have also bred student irresponsibility by sidetracking us. By putting so much emphasis on subject matter and skills, many educators seem to have lost sight of the fact that good teachers always have fostered learning in many directions — mastery of subject, intellectual skills, personal behavior, values. Idealistically, and perhaps naively, we believed in the past that we were preparing students not only for jobs but for their places in the larger world. In the liberal arts, we have justified our existence in a society intent on cost-effectiveness by claiming that we were educating the whole human being for Life, not merely training a brain for a skill. Those of us in history have liked the Jeffersonian model — we were producing responsible citizens for the well-being of the republic, for the greater social good.

I still believe in all that — and I think most educators do. We just have concentrated so hard on stating clear objectives and providing a supportive, non-threatening environment for students that we have de-emphasized values and personal behavior. It's often too much trouble to write objectives for values. Are they objectives or goals? How do you put them in behavioral terms? What will the measurable outcome be? Better to forget it.

In a complex, heterogeneous society that speeds through social change at a dizzying pace, one cannot blame education alone for the lack of emphasis on values. Increasingly, however, the literature on curriculum development calls for ways to teach values once again, and to teach students to define and assess their own values.

In recent years, the definition of values has become so political — involving race, sex, religion — that we seem to have forgotten that some values are just practical, common-sense attributes that pay off directly in our personal and professional lives. Responsibility toward our families, our employers, and our communities permits us to function as true adults with ultimately greater freedom. Self-discipline gives us a rein on personal wants and passions so that we can command a responsive body and mind. A mind that does what its owner tells it to do is a precious thing.

Our students need such values. They will work at jobs in which their bosses cannot — or choose not to — define objectives and expectations for them. They will encounter some employers who demand the highest standards — and others who perform so shabbily that the employees' only recourse for self-respect is in the standards they set for themselves.

I know most students eventually learn some of all this. The marketplace, particularly in a depressed economy, teaches them. But why should they have to be fired twice to learn?

We must go beyond the pedagogy of skills and quantitative objectives and once again profess our own values through our behavior and through our expectations for our students. We teach values when we refuse to tolerate procrastination, self-indulgence, laziness, or lack of any sense of priorities. We can encourage students to make decisions about what is important to them, and we can give them the tools and guidelines to make those decisions.

Without sacrificing the gains we have made through modern teaching strategies and without losing compassion, we must force students to practice self-discipline and to take responsibility for their own learning.

Students' Rights and the Teacher's Obligations in the Classroom

Conwell G. Strickland

Ed.'s Note: Although this article was published 15 years ago, the points seem as valid in 1990 as they were in 1975.

The college student of the '70s is demanding his rights. He insists on the right to protest. He is demanding to be included on governing boards and committees which deal with the governance of the institution. He wants to select the speakers and the entertainers who visit the campus. Most of these demands center on the administration of the institutions of higher learning.

In another area of life on the campus, that of classroom procedure, the student has not been so demanding — and yet from this realm stems much of the dissatisfaction which has led to unrest among students. A major complaint is that curriculum content is not relevant. Another is that too often classes are taught by graduate assistants rather than by full-time faculty personnel. Too many faculty members devote too much of what is supposed to be instructional time to personal research or to speaking engagements concerning their research. Many students complain that they lose their personal identity in a jumble of social security numbers, registration numbers, and seat and row numbers, and are never considered as individual personalities. In addition to making these complaints, some students are beginning to give attention to the methods and procedures used by the faculty in the classroom. On one campus the student congress adopted a resolution requesting the faculty to adopt measures that would decrease the emphasis on memorizing facts as the major learning activity in which they engage. Against such a background of criticism and protest it seems worthwhile to consider the rights of the student in the classroom.

The American citizen has the strength of the Constitution to guarantee that he receive his rights. The student does not have such a force concerning his rights as a learner. He has to depend primarily on the individual faculty member to see that the classroom procedure provides the "just claims" to which the student is entitled. In the business of higher education the student is the customer, and as in any other business, attention needs to be given to satisfying the demands of the customer. It is possible that in higher education the customer is not always right, but surely the student should be allowed some reasonable expectations which fall within the realm of faculty responsibility.

Too often the just claims of the student are overlooked by the pressure of large enrollments and the automated processes necessary for handling the registrations of large student populations. The individual faculty member, with the demands made on his time and the administrative policies within which he works, often fails to give sufficient recognition to the students in his classes. Regardless of such conditions, the major business of the institution is instruction. Regardless of other functions the institution may carry on — research, community service, publication — the major responsibility of higher education is to the student. The school that responds to this responsibility will give attention to the students' instructional needs as well as to the protests and criticisms of its students. The key person in meeting this responsibility is the individual faculty member, and the responsibility will be best met in the setting of the classroom.

Students' rights may be organized and stated in different ways. An attempt is made not to reflect all of the desires of students, but to include those most frequently expressed. My impressions have come from personal experience, observations about the informal discussions with students, the frequently reported demands of students, and the content of contemporary literature concerning higher education.

The student has a right to be recognized as an individual. This first right of the student stems from a basic democratic value, the dignity of the individual. Large enrollments and the concomitant large-group lecture sections do not allow for such recognition. However, in the normal-sized class the teacher can know his students by name, not merely by a row and seat number on a seating chart. It is doubtful that any other practice is appreciated more by students than the attempt on the part of the teacher to learn the names of his students.

The student is entitled to a faculty member interested in teaching. Enthusiasm is catching. The teacher who is not interested in what he is doing cannot generate enthusiasm in his students. When the faculty member is working under undue pressures to do research, subject to "publish or perish" pressures regarding promotion and tenure or other such administrative policies, it is sometimes difficult to give full attention to teaching. When the student is forced to spend class time participating in the instructor's research, often unrelated to the immediate course, his time is not being devoted to the purposes for which he is enrolled. Also, the course can become very boring when research statistics are substituted for basic content.

The student is entitled to instruction based on adequate preparation. Until recent years very little attention has been given to methodology in teaching at the college or university level. The lecture has long been the accepted method of instruction. However, even a well-prepared lecture does not always mean adequate preparation. Mere presentation of information is not sufficient for the modern classroom. Our present knowledge of the process of learning indicates that many students do not have backgrounds adequate for a full understanding of what is being presented in the lecture. It is necessary to consider the immediate class personnel in order to provide sufficient explanation and illustration to make the lecture more meaningful.

A corollary to adequate preparation is use of the wide variety of instructional media now available to the instructor. The college instructor utilizes teaching materials and aids less than teachers at any other level of the educational system. No longer is it necessary to limit classroom procedure to the lecture. Instructional technology has advanced to such an extent that there are media available for use in all of the disciplines. The college student should not be deprived of these advantages.

Students have a right to express opinions and to challenge those of the instructor. It has been said that one of the purposes of education is to develop thinking, participating, decision-making citizens. In many instances the college student is never given the opportunity to evaluate or to criticize the information presented to him in a course. If the teacher accepts the responsibility to assist the student in thinking and decision-making, he will provide the opportunity for the student to express opinions and to challenge those stated in the lecture or discussion. It is a valuable experience for the student to be confronted with situations in which he is required to formulate opinions and to defend his ideas with evidence. He needs to be challenged to have sound bases for any opinion expressed. This type of activity will assist the student in learning to distinguish between fact and fiction, and fact and opinion, and how to deal with controversial content.

A well-known writer and teacher told a group in an informal conversation that dealing with the controversial in teaching offers no problems to the teacher who can recognize the difference between fact and opinion. Because of the wide variety of viewpoints and the controversial content in many of the disciplines this kind of challenge and confrontation is possible in the college classroom.

Instruction should be individualized. Statements concerning the individualization of instruction, personalizing education for the student, making teaching more relevant, and similar declarations fill the literature and echo from the speaker's platform. Institutions of higher learning are being surveyed by governmental agencies and private foundations for evidence that such ideas are being put into practice. In spite of these efforts, the typical assignments for most college courses tend to contradict this contemporary emphasis on individualized teaching. Most students are still being greeted on the first day of class each semester with assignments to study the text, read so many pages of collateral reading, attend a given number of laboratory sessions, write a research paper, and take a certain number of tests. College students are capable of and have a right to differentiated assignments. This change may bring about some variation in evaluation procedures, cause some criticism from colleagues, or even result in expressions of horror by some concerning the effect on the grading curve. The major concern should be what will happen to the student, not what happens to traditional practice.

The student is entitled to access to the teacher at hours other than class time. The relationship of the faculty member to his students is an important facet of teaching. Students wish to talk with their teachers for various reasons. Some seek advice from time to time, some wish to make a comment or raise a question they would not bring up in the class, while others may wish to come in for a brief chat. One new student on campus entered the office, introduced himself, and when asked by the professor if there was anything he could do for him, replied, "Well, sir, I do not have class with you. I had heard about you, and ... uh ... uh ... well, I guess I just wanted to meet you." To some this might be considered a waste of the teacher's time. Yet, to some students it is important that they feel free to enter a teacher's office and talk with him. This is not to suggest that faculty members be required to maintain a set number of office hours. It has been my experience that an administrative policy requiring office hours for the faculty usually is the result of the faculty's failure to make time available to their students. Association with students is one of the more pleasant rewards of teaching.

The student is entitled to know the system by which he is to be graded. The emphasis placed on high grades by society, especially the academic segment of society, places the student under heavy pressure. At best, he can be apprised of the standards by which he is to be evaluated and the system by which he is being graded. This needs to be done at the beginning of the course. The institution likely has in the catalogue a general policy statement concerning grading. Within the framework of the policy each faculty member determines the actual grading procedure. Probably the only absolute requirement of the faculty member is to report his grades according to a letter grading system. Outside of this general requirement lies a wide variation of practice among instructors.

The student has a right to attend or not to attend class. This is probably the most controversial of the rights expressed. Many students feel that there should not be an attendance requirement for any class. Their point of view is that if they can successfully complete the course without class attendance, they should be allowed to do so. The teacher's counterargument might be to make the class sessions so important to the course and so interesting that the student will feel that he will miss something worthwhile if he fails to attend.

Students have a right to evaluate their courses and teacher. Evaluation of faculty by students is an accepted practice on major college campuses today. It is good to know if a course has contributed something to the student and just how competent the instructor appears to his students. Many faculty members who oppose student evaluation rightly argue that there is a close correlation between grades the student makes and the ratings given the teacher. However, this does not cancel all of the value of student evaluation of the faculty. Students are going to evaluate their teachers from the very first day of a class. Some student organizations on campus prepare and distribute evaluation sheets on individual faculty members. Since this appears to be a universal practice among students, an organized system for student evaluations should bring increased benefits to the faculty member who uses the results as a basis for his own self-evaluation for the purposes of improvement.

To conclude, students are demanding more and more of institutions of higher learning and their faculties. Recognition of their demands and a careful evaluation of them can provide a sound basis for needed improvement in the educational system. Right or wrong, the students' views could be worth considering.

Ethical Standards in Teaching

Wilbert J. McKeachie

As part of the code of ethics for psychologists, the American Psychological Association has published a code of ethics for teachers of psychology. Those portions relevant for all college teachers follow:

"The teacher should encourage students in their quest for knowledge, giving them every assistance in the free exploration of ideas. Teaching frequently and legitimately involves a presentation of disquieting facts and controversial theories, and it is in the examination of perplexing issues that students most need the guidance of a good teacher. Disturbing concepts should not be withheld from students simply because some individuals may be distressed by them. When issues are relevant, they should be given full and objective discussion so that students can make intelligent decisions with regard to them. However, presentation of ideas likely to be difficult for some students to accept should be governed by tact and respect for the worth of the individual."

"Differing approaches to one's discipline should be presented to students in such a way as to encourage them to study the relevant facts and draw their own conclusions. Free expression of both criticism and support of the various approaches is to be encouraged as essential to the development of individual students and the field. In dealing with an area of specialization other than his or her own, a teacher should make it clear that he or she is not speaking as a specialist. In attempting to make an understandable and interesting presentation of subject matter to students, an instructor should not sacrifice adequacy of treatment to considerations of popular appeal."

"A teacher should respect students' right to privacy and not require students to give information which they may wish to withhold; neither should the teacher reveal information which a student has given with the reasonable assumption that it will be held in confidence."

"A teacher should require of students only activities which are designed to contribute to the student in the area of instruction. Other activities not related to course objectives and not having secondary values should be made available to students on a voluntary basis. Exploitation of students to obtain research data or assistance with the teacher's own work is unethical."

"Faculty members advising students electing their own field as a major field of study with the intent of entering the profession should be sure that students understand opportunities and requirements in the field, e.g., that few positions are open to those with only a bachelor's degree. that there is considerable screening of candidates at the graduate level, that the doctorate is required for many positions (and that academic positions are scarce in the 1980s)."

"A teacher who becomes aware of an adjustment problem in a student who might profit by counseling or psychotherapy should assist the student to find such help if it is available. When a student requests assistance, and counseling facilities are not available, the nonclinically trained instructor may offer help as an immediate expedient. In doing so he or she should indicate to the student that he or she is acting not as a trained counselor or clinical psychologist but simply as a teacher interested in the student's welfare. Teachers should not enter into counseling relationships with students for a fee."

Interestingly enough the APA statement, which was one of the earliest codes of ethics dealing with academic behavior, does not deal with one of the most salient current issues — sexual harassment. Sexual harassment as defined in my university is:

Unwelcome sexual advances, requests for sexual favors, and other verbal or physical conduct of a sexual nature constitute sexual harassment when

- submission to such conduct is made either explicitly or implicitly a term or condition of an individual's employment or education;

- submission to or rejection of such conduct by an individual is used as the basis for academic or employment decisions affecting that individual;

- such conduct has the purpose or effect of substantially interfering with an individual's academic or professional performance or creating an intimidating, hostile or offensive employment, education, or living environment.

Sexual harassment is illegal under both Michigan and U.S. law.

Supplementary Reading

Many other disciplines have ethical codes. I suggest that you review the code of your own discipline. Most of us aren't even aware of the code until we, or some colleagues, are accused of a violation. In the area of sexual harassment, a good book — despite its title — is by Billie Wright Dzich and Linda Winer: *The Lecherous Professor* (Boston: Beacon Press, 1984).

SECTION 2

Introduction: As You Plan for Your First Course

Achieving Excellence: Advice to New Teachers
by M. Neil Browne and Stuart M. Keeley

Syllabus Shares "What the Teacher Wants"
by Howard B. Altman
from *The Teaching Professor*, May 1989

The Textbook Selection Checklist
developed by Brian Hemmings and David Battersby

Blackboards and Overheads
by Maryellen Weimer
from *The Teaching Professor*, March and April 1987

Meeting a Class for the First Time
by Wilbert J. McKeachie

As You Plan for Your First Course

Now it's time to get down to details. For most teachers the novelty of the new position wears off upon receipt of the actual teaching assignment. Then the realization dawns, "I'm going to be in class this time tomorrow (next week, next month) — and I don't have a ghost of an idea what I'm going to do."

The planning process varies greatly, dependent on the nature of the teaching assignment. Teaching assistants typically instruct as part of a larger course. They do labs, recitation sections, discussion groups or problem-solving review sessions. They do not design a course, select a textbook, figure out the course grading policy or decide how fast to pace the content. That sounds desirable, if you don't have much lead time before the class starts or aren't as familiar as you might be with the content, but this situation is not without planning dilemmas of its own. How does what you're suppose to do "fit" with the rest of the course? What if the pace turns out to be too fast for the students? What if you don't agree with the grading policy or can't believe what turned up on the final (which you saw for the first time when you passed it out)? Some of what appears in this section might not be relevant to teaching assistants. All of what appears in Section 1 is, as is most in Sections 3 and 4.

Part-time faculty are frequently hired to teach an already existing course. Here what's prescribed is the content to be covered. Often syllabi from other sections may be available for review, as are lists of previously used texts. Frequently, part-timers can make more decisions than TAs. They do put together a syllabus for the course and make decisions about assignments, textbooks, and grading policies. They don't teach in response to what somebody else has covered, but face the consequences of their instructional decisions alone.

Full-time faculty make the same kind of decisions as part-timers, although in some cases they do design brand new courses, starting from scratch, so to speak, in terms of having to make decisions and prepare materials. In addition, new faculty teach a full load, which means all the planning decisions necessary for a single course must be made two, three or four times, depending on the number of courses taught. Part-timers do frequently teach full-time, but they don't usually get their spate of new courses all at once.

All of which leads us to suggest that new college teachers need first to determine the degree to which the course(s) they'll be teaching need to be planned. With the task clearly in mind, decisions as to what to read in this section are easier. We do recommend that everyone start with the first article — which may at first reading seem not to fit well with the focus of the section, although it begins with an almost unbeatable appeal. This is the advice two seasoned veterans wish somebody had offered them when they were "neophytes." What doesn't seem to fit with the section focus is the advice: "Ask frequent questions during each class," "Explicitly teach and encourage the development of mental skills that transcend memory," "Require students to acknowledge the problems identified by your evaluation of their work," and so on. (pp. 39-43) Sure, these are things teachers do when they teach, but classroom activities like these must be planned.

We submit that one of the reasons faculty have so much trouble getting students to participate in class is found in the kind and quality of questions asked. In the classroom, like most other places, the quality of the question to no small degree influences the quality of the answer. If you want to teach students to do more than memorize information, you must plan classroom activities and events that encourage this kind of higher-order learning. These are indeed questions of planning. We recommend you start the planning process by envisioning the class as you want to teach it. With that vision in mind, you then back up and work on your syllabus, select your text, and figure out what you're going to do on the blackboard and/or overhead.

Finally, we recommend the last reading in the section, for everyone as well. All teachers meet a class for the first time. McKeachie wisely observes, "The first class meeting, like any other situation in which you are meeting a group of strangers who will affect your well-being, is at the same time exciting and anxiety-producing for both students and teacher." (p. 51) First impressions do matter. The stakes are high on the first day. How do you make yours the class students discuss with excitement at dinner?

Course planning issues affect every aspect of teaching — you will discover the extent to which in your first teaching experience. Other topics ought to be included in the section, but we suspect at this moment you're not as interested in reading about planning course details as you are in making those nuts-and-bolts decisions. Think about them, not just in terms of material in this section, but in light of what has proceeded and is about to follow.

Achieving Excellence: Advice to New Teachers

M. Neil Browne and Stuart M. Keeley

New teachers, fresh with enthusiasm, deserve better advice than most educational research provides. Disputes about effective teaching are fueled by strong views on alternative models of teaching. While these disagreements are significant, they divert our energies away from techniques or behaviors that are embraced by most experienced teachers. Despite a consensus about behavior that contributes to superior teaching,[1] most research that focuses on the teaching process is *descriptive*, rather than *prescriptive*. Typically, such studies shy away from establishing a link between specific teacher behavior and probable educational outcome.

This article makes some suggestions for new teachers who aspire to excellence. Our suggestions stem from our experiences as teachers in our respective disciplines and in interdisciplinary programs (Eble, 1983). Our numerous encounters with dedicated teachers expanded our appreciation for the shared prescriptions that developed from our personal classroom experience. While it seems pretentious to attempt a list of behaviors consistent with excellent teaching, we wish that experienced teachers might have provided us with just this type of advice when we were neophytes. Those who share our concern for the perils of the non-directive on-the-job training procedure encountered by most new teachers can supplement or delete elements of our list. But experienced teachers know more about their craft than we sometimes pretend. While new teachers should have broad latitude to experiment and create, they should also be aware that some teaching behaviors are particularly productive. Those of us who serve as role models for new teachers have a responsibility to identify those behaviors.

A few caveats should precede these suggestions.

First, certain suggestions are more appropriate for some courses than others. Large classrooms have special problems that may minimize the utility of individual suggestions. In addition, those courses where the primary objective is either memorizing a huge volume of accepted facts or acquiring a technical vocabulary would be inappropriate contexts for those suggestions aimed at classrooms with broader educational objectives.

Second, while most elements on our list would be compatible with contending visions of teaching excellence, we owe it to the reader to make our major pedagogical assumptions explicit.

- Initially, we assume that interactive learning is preferable to passive learning.

- Next, we make the related assumption that the development of critical thinking skills is as important a goal as content acquisition.

- Finally, we assume that demanding mental effort is painful in the short run, but highly satisfying in the long run. This final assumption requires the attendant belief that respect from students is preferable to their immediate approval. Ideally, of course, it is especially desirable to engender both short-run applause and long-run gratitude from students.

A third qualification to our suggestions is the omission of those forms of advice that are already relatively obvious to the new instructor. Certainly, nervous gestures should be eliminated; lectures should be orderly; notes on blackboards should be legible. However, achieving these minimal standards hardly places the new instructor on the path toward teaching excellence. Each of our suggestions is comparatively more difficult then the mechanics mentioned above; but the type of learning they encourage provides unusually satisfying rewards.

The next section consists of advice to new teachers who wish to be excellent teachers. Our list of suggestions is in no particular order. Each suggestion strikes us as important in its own right, but a teacher who tries to implement individual suggestions would probably miss the holistic strength of the entire set. The final section proposes the modification of student evaluation forms so that they focus on the elements of teaching excellence.

Suggestions for Better Teaching

Ask frequent questions during each class

Students will think when you require them to do so. It would be nice to enter a classroom where students would of their own volition struggle with intellectually demanding tasks. In fact, there are a very few students who do conform to that romantic characterization. Students rarely think intensely for the same reason that professors primarily lecture. It is relatively secure and simple to stay with behavior patterns that are familiar and non-threatening.

If you ask questions frequently, you must be patient. If students notice that the teacher after a brief pause answers each question he asks, students will soon wait until the teacher answers his own questions. Such a pattern transforms what appears at first glance to be questioning behavior into a mode of lecturing. Hence, new teachers should generally hesitate to answer questions they ask until their students have had adequate opportunity to experiment with a response. The patience required is difficult to develop because responsible teachers want to "cover" a lot. Thus, every silence of extended duration subtracts from lecture material that the teacher could have delivered.

What seems faulty about this quest for "coverage" is that it presumes that when teachers speak, others learn (Glaser, 1968). Those of us who regularly wince at the test results of our own students should know better than to make this assumption. Moreover, when a teacher covers an extensive body of material, the teacher's behavior has not thereby developed complex cognitive skills for students.

There are several excellent sources for teachers who want to improve their ability to develop effective questions (Dillon, 1982). Payne (1951), for instance, has some good advice on the treatment of respondents to questions so as to maximize the type of desired responses. Hunkins (1972), Browne and Keeley (1981), and Saunders (1966) all provide useful discussions on levels and purposes of classroom questions. Instructors at any stage of development might benefit from a review of the 25 questioning dialogues that Hyman (1979) developed as models of questioning behavior.

Ask only those questions that will inform you about what the student is learning

Asking just any question is not necessarily more advantageous than asking no question at all. Questions which require students to apply their assignments or make reasoned judgments about the worth of a particular contention require complex thought at the same time that they provide feedback to the instructor about the effectiveness of her performance as a teacher. Answers to such questions advance the understanding of everyone in the classroom. They indicate individual problems, provide an opportunity for creativity, and reveal to the teacher the actual level of learning that has transpired.

Teachers frequently deceive themselves into believing that more learning is occurring than a realistic appraisal would find. McKeachie (1980) and Entwistle and Ramsden (1983) help teachers understand that students process information at a different pace and in different forms than teachers disseminate it. Eble (1981) and Davies (1983) have both pointed out how tempting and erroneous it is to assume that students are learning while the teacher is teaching. They want their students to learn; there is always a small coterie of students who look as if they might be learning; hopes concerning student achievements are easily transformed into beliefs that these achievements do exist. Evidence for these exaggerated beliefs that students have learned what they have been taught may be derived from student answers to ineffective questions from their instructors.

Teachers may habitually ask their students the following set of relatively wasteful questions:

- Does everyone understand?

- Have I made myself clear?

- Are there any questions?

The modal response to each of these questions is silence. The questions are treated by students as a ritualistic exercise by teachers. So rare is a student response to these questions that asking them has only slightly more educational value than asking no question at all. When students do not answer such questions, learning should not be inferred.

A deficiency in each of the three ineffective questions listed above is the ease with which they can be answered with a "yes" or "no." When students are permitted to answer a question by silence or by uttering a one-word reply, the teacher has little appreciation for what the student's response actually means. Such responses are too brief and ambiguous to provide accurate sketches of what has or has not been learned.

Questions that require lengthier, more complex answers enable both teacher and learner to decipher the impact of a particular learning experience. Examples of these more effective types of questions are the following:

- What is your understanding of ...?

- How would you evaluate ...?

- Why was X included in the text, lecture, or argument?

Require students to ask precise questions

It is difficult to give disciplined answers to lazy questions. Teachers and students both experience frustration when a student says, "I'm lost. Can you help me with Chapter 23?" The teacher needs a more precise question to be helpful. A student may not be able immediately to form a description of the problem he is having. Students will not be aware of this difficulty if the teacher does not address it directly with them. Students can be encouraged by excellent teachers to delight in the self-discipline required to formulate a question that can be meaningfully answered.

When students are permitted to follow their normal inclinations, they will ask vague questions that do indicate confusion, but offer no apparent pathway whereby that condition can be repaired. Questions such as "Could you clarify Chapter 10?" or "Would you please go over theory X?" are frustrating because a serious attempt to respond might take three class periods.

Students can expedite their own understanding and enhance the efficiency of the class by asking questions that focus directly on the problem they are experiencing. By requiring students to use a format such as "My understanding of theory X is .... Is that correct?", you can determine whether anything about theory X is understood, particular elements need clarification, or the student is ready to advance to subsequent material.

In general we find it useful to respond to whatever question a student asks by asking the student to first explain his or her present understanding. When students are taught to reflect before they ask questions, they will find themselves actively engaging with the course material. In addition, they will find that teachers really can answer their queries in an enriching fashion.

Explicitly teach and encourage the development of mental skills that transcend memory

To facilitate the type of self-censorial behavior that post-school learning requires, teachers should require students to practice the evaluative and synthetic skills that will permit them to build on the knowledge they have accumulated while in school (Browne and Keeley, 1981). That is, it is important that students practice actively asking questions about course material. Unfortunately, this usually means that you have to explain gradually the meaning of these questioning skills for the student, since the majority of classrooms will not demand their use (Barnes, 1983; Fischer and Grant, 1983).

Many of the skills that transcend memory are rarely taught in classrooms, except in an indirect fashion. Thus, the teacher who hopes to cultivate those skills must not only ask questions in class and on tests that encourage the use of these skills, she must also teach the skills explicitly. These skills are spelled out in some detail in a number of texts (Browne and Keeley, 1981; Carlson, 1978). Skills that transcend memory include:

- the identification of ambiguity and assumptions,

- judgments about the quality of evidence and inferences,

- recognition of significant omitted information, and

- the formulation of decisions based on personal value commitments and reasonable arguments.

Teachers can do several things to stimulate higher-order thinking processes in students (Cooper, 1977). First, teachers themselves can familiarize themselves with the skills by reviewing critical thinking texts. A second technique is to distribute to and review with the students at the beginning of the course a list of critical questions to ask about materials. The third is to require the student to actively use this list through homework assignments and through classroom questioning activities. It is important frequently to remind the student to "keep your eye on the list" while studying. We have found the following set of questions particularly useful (Browne, Haas, and Keeley, 1978):

- What is the conclusion or main point?

- What are the reasons or evidence?

- What are the elements of ambiguity?

- What assumptions are being made?
- How convincing are the reasons or evidence?
- What value priorities are evident?
- Is there important missing information?

Higher-order mental skills are developed by no particular department or course. They are considered every teacher's responsibility. Hence, they are typically overlooked as the teacher plans her classroom activities around those topics for which she has been assigned specific responsibility by her colleagues. An excellent teacher must resist this tendency to ignore high-order mental skills, and the primary path of resistance is to teach students explicitly how to analyze, integrate, and evaluate.

Share your performance objectives with your students

Picture in your mind what an ideal student performance would look like, then prepare your instructions for assignments and tests. If you are fuzzy in your own mind about the behavior expected, the student is forced to play a guessing game. There is nothing particularly exemplary about guessing correctly and excelling on such an assignment. Those assignments with behavioral clarity offer a real opportunity for a more equitable assessment of student performance.

Provide students with alternative models, visions, or interpretations

These optional viewpoints or interpretations alert learners to the many questions about which reasonable people frequently disagree. In addition, they tempt the learner to risk personal commitment, to make a judgment. One of the most memorable events for any learner must be when he recognizes that learning is so much more complex than is suggested by simply mastering knowledge. It is exciting to enter a shared quest for better answers on a personal level; it is tedious to memorize and apply pat answers sanctioned by the experts in the domain.

Take frequent breaks in lectures or discussions to ask students to summarize or explain the significance of what was just said

There is an enormous chasm between what is said in a class and what the student hears or infers. Both the student and teacher need feedback about the specifics of that discrepancy. In classroom discussions this technique is particularly effective as a means of encouraging students to listen to one another. Most students know they are supposed to listen to teachers, but they are reluctant to focus attention on the statements of "just another student." Such an attitude is deadly to the classroom that relies on productive student interchanges. One benefit of forcing students to put into words their interpretation of the significance of what was just said is the possibility that their notes will be improved. A useful device for integrating notes from a course is the habit of jotting down why a certain topic is being discussed at that particular juncture of the course.

Require students to acknowledge the problems identified by your evaluation of their work

One of the most onerous tasks of the teacher, but also one of the potentially most rewarding, is the evaluation of students' exams and papers. This evaluation optimally should provide information that students can use to improve feedback during the course (Carlson, 1978). Thus, for essay assignments, specific written comments or ratings assigned to specific criteria are superior to holistic ratings, such as an overall grade. While many forms of specific feedback can contribute to learning, many students cannot use feedback in a corrective fashion unless the teacher takes explicit steps to require such action. In the absence of these explicit evaluative comments, students' initial reactions usually consist of noting that the teacher is indicating something good or bad about their performance. If the learner is to use feedback in a corrective fashion, then he must think carefully about each comment the teacher made on the exam or paper.

One technique for increasing the likelihood that grading will be the learning experience that it can be is to incorporate the idea that an assignment or test is not completed when you return the paper or exam to the student. Instead, your comments on the returned work include an imperative for ongoing communication between the student and you. For instance, the student might be required to provide you with a rationale for each of the positive comments on her paper and a correction plus rationale for the correction for each of the negative comments. By attempting to understand what about certain aspects of her work was so positive that she received compliments, the student can replicate those tendencies on future assignments. By correcting negative comments, the student can focus on what she did not know before or on elements of her work about which she should become more precise.

Further good examples of how to provide useful feedback are provided by Carlson (1978). Also, the *Handbook of Formative and Summative Evaluation of Student Learning* (1971) gives a useful description of how to design tests for feedback.

Share with students your rationale for unique classroom behavior

Presenting at the outset explicit statements of your values, of your basic assumptions about the educational process, and of how your "different" teaching procedures can help them reach desirable educational goals, helps create a feeling in the learners that they are getting something special and unique. Since efforts to become an outstanding teacher will by definition distinguish you as "different," you might as well acknowledge the designation and turn it to your advantage. Students repeatedly indicate that they learn more from those who evince enthusiasm and concern for the quality of teaching, even though they may frequently complain about their own required extra effort. Thus, it is helpful to provide them an explanation for your systematic efforts to enrich the learning process. Such an explanation provides you with a dual opportunity to demonstrate to students that you have carefully reflected about what you are doing as a teacher and to explain exactly why you have adopted the format they are experiencing.

Improving Student Evaluation Forms

The effectiveness of teachers is frequently gauged by student evaluation forms. The forms typically contain questions about the curriculum materials chosen by the teacher as well as questions inquiring about the teacher's clarity, organization, empathy, and knowledge. Most significantly, the forms contain a global rating of the instructor. Such a summary assessment does not serve diagnostic or formative purposes because the instructor does not know the rationale for the score (Eble, 1983). This last item is especially controversial because it provides a convenient number by which administrators can rate teachers.

What rankles many sensitive teachers about this ranking system is first the murkiness of the criteria used by students to determine the global rating. A second legitimate concern about ratings is the association between favorable ratings and factors such as high prior subject interest, higher expected grades, and lower levels of difficulty (Marsh, 1983). These correlates of high ratings may be either educationally unsound or beyond the instructor's control.

Reliance on the global rating as the single indicator of teaching performance is based on an overly rational model. Somehow the untrained rater implicitly reviews the relevant (unnamed) criteria and arrives at a reasonable weighted average prior to his designation of the global ranking. The hurried and superficial procedure for filling out these important evaluation forms seems inconsistent with the heavy weight given such forms by administrators.

Despite their flaws, student evaluation forms will be around for a while. Professors are reluctant to evaluate the teaching of their peers in any systematic fashion. Teaching performance needs to be evaluated. Students are viewing the teacher on a regular basis. Consequently, they are and doubtlessly will continue to be the raters of teacher quality. Nearly 70% of colleges now use student evaluations as a major source of information about teaching. This number represents a 35% increase from 10 years ago (Seldin, 1983).

How can student ratings of teacher performance be improved? One obvious, but unrealistic, improvement would result from a training program for the raters (Keeley and Browne, 1978; Pulich, 1984). Without a well-conceived idea of the characteristics of teaching excellence, the raters must rely on whatever comes to mind at the point of evaluation. Since training programs for student raters are impractical, the form should highlight those factors that constitute high quality teaching. To a minor extent current forms do make that attempt. However, their concern for clarity and organization call to the raters' attention only those aspects of teaching that provide a floor on the definition of acceptable teaching.

The criteria on rating forms should include questions that teach or remind the student that excellent teaching is much more than a coherent presentation to a class. To the extent that rating forms refer raters to specific behavior rather than to lists of traits, the results will be less ambiguous (Pulich, 1984).

The list of behavioral suggestions for excellent teaching contained in this article provides one possible set of questions, the inclusion of which would improve the acceptability and quality of student evaluations. Even if a colleague has low regard for our particular suggestions, he or she may see the need to modify student evaluations in the manner we are proposing. If teachers are to be rated by their students, the evaluations should be based on someone's reflective definition of teaching excellence. Current forms rely heavily on a pedestrian and bureaucratic concept of what a teacher can accomplish.

Notes

[1] While this article focuses on teacher behavior, we are convinced that excellent teaching also requires an awareness of the significance of style or presence. What one *is* in the classroom is often as important as what one *does*.

References

Barnes, C.P. "Questioning in College Classrooms." In Ellner, C.L., & Barnes, C.P., *Studies of College Teaching*. Lexington, MA: Lexington Books, 1983.

Bloom, B.S.; Hastings, J.T.; & Madaus, G.F. *Handbook on Formative and Summative Evaluation of Student Learning*. New York: McGraw-Hill, 1971.

Browne, M.N., & Keeley, S.M. *Asking the Right Questions*. Englewood Cliffs, NJ: Prentice-Hall, 1981.

Browne, M.N.; Haas, P.F.; & Keeley, S.M. "Measuring Critical Thinking Skills in College." *Educational Forum*, 42 (1978): 219-226.

Carlson, C.R. "Feedback for Learning." In Milton, O., *On College Teaching*. San Francisco: Jossey-Bass, 1978.

Cooper, J.M. *Classroom Teaching Skills: A Handbook*. Lexington, MA: D.C. Heath, 1977.

Davies, L.J. "Teaching University Students How to Learn." *Improving College and University Teaching*, 31 (1983): 160-165.

Dillon, J.T. "The Multidisciplinary Study of Questioning." *Journal of Educational Psychology*, 74 (1982): 147-165.

Eble, K. *The Aim of the College Teacher*. San Francisco: Jossey-Bass, 1983.

Eble, K. *The Craft of Teaching*. San Francisco: Jossey-Bass, 1981.

Entwistle, N.J., & Ramsden, P. *Understanding Student Learning*. New York: Nichols Publishing, 1983.

Fischer, C.G., & Grant, G.E. "Intellectual Levels in College Classrooms." In Ellner, C.L., & Barnes, C.P., *Studies of College Teaching*. Lexington, MA: Lexington Books, 1983.

Glaser, R. "Ten Untenable Assumptions of College Instruction." *Education Record*, 49 (1968): 154-159.

Hunkins, F.P. *Questioning Strategies and Techniques*. Boston: Allyn and Bacon, 1972.

Hyman, R.T. *Strategic Questioning*. Englewood Cliffs, NJ: Prentice-Hall, 1979.

Keeley, S.M., & Browne, M.N. "Improving Student Evaluation Forms: Related Need for Critical Thinking Emphasis and Trained Raters." *Peabody Journal of Education*, 55 (1978): 305-308.

Marsh, H.W. "Multidimensional Ratings of Teaching Effectiveness by Students from Different Academic Settings and Their Relation to Student/Course/Instructor Characteristics." *Journal of Education Psychology*, 75 (1983): 150-166.

McKeachie, W.J. "Improving Lectures by Understanding Students' Information Processing." In *New Directions for Teaching and Learning*. San Francisco: Jossey-Bass, 1980.

Murray, H.G. "Low-Inference Classroom Teaching Behaviors and Student Ratings of College Teaching Effectiveness." *Journal of Education Psychology*, 75 (1983): 138-149.

Payne, S.L. *The Art of Asking Questions*. Princeton, NJ: Princeton University Press, 1951.

Pulich, M.A. "Better Use of Student Evaluations for Teaching Effectiveness." *Improving College and University Teaching*, 32 (1984): 91-94.

Sanders, N.M. *Classroom Questions*. New York: Harper and Row, 1966.

Seldin, P. "How American Colleges Evaluate Teaching." Abstracts of contributed papers, Improving University Teaching, Ninth International Conference, Dublin, Ireland (1983): 155.

Syllabus Shares "What the Teacher Wants"

Howard B. Altman

Robert Mager prefaces his book, *Preparing Instructional Objectives*, with a fable about a seahorse who sets out to find his fortune without a plan for getting there. To be sure, the seahorse fails to wind up where he had hoped. In the "real world" of the higher education classroom, so do many students, and possibly more than a few faculty, fail to get where they want to go.

The purpose of a syllabus is to let students and faculty know where they will "wind up." It achieves its purpose only when it provides sufficient information to followers: the path they are on, the obstacles they must overcome, the requirements they are expected to meet and the kinds of evidence which document that they have "wound up" where they were supposed to.

Too many faculty equate a course syllabus with an *outline of course topics*, a *calendar of dates* when each will be covered, and a *list of readings* to be done for each topic. While such information is *part* of a syllabus, it is *only* part. The whole of the information which learners need is considerably more.

A syllabus constitutes a *legal written covenant* between faculty member and students. It binds students, who wish to succeed in a course, to a path they should follow, and also binds the instructor to the same path. If instructors wish to change the path, this is their prerogative — but that change becomes part of a revised syllabus and must be communicated in writing.

A model syllabus contains:

1. Personal Information

This section serves as the preface and includes the course name, course code number, number of credits, day(s) and time(s) when it meets, as well as the location where the course is held.

It includes the instructor's name, office location, the office hours, and the office telephone number(s). If the instructor chooses to list a home telephone number, indicate the restrictions on its use (e.g., "not after 11 p.m., please").

2. Course Description

This section provides a brief description of the nature of the course, generally corresponding to that supplied officially in the college catalog, where appropriate.

3. Course Objectives

This section indicates the general or specific objectives to which the instructor will be teaching and which students are expected to achieve. Performance statements detail what students are expected to be able to do by the end of the course that they couldn't do at the beginning. Short-term objectives as well as terminal ones may be listed in this section. Here are a few sample objectives, taken from the author's "Introduction to Linguistics" course:

- "Students will be able to recognize symbols of the International Phonetic Alphabet (IPA) and do phonetic transcriptions of simple English sentences using the IPA."

- "Students will become familiar with the notation system used to illustrate structural relations and will be able to construct tree diagrams for sentences which illustrate specific syntactic rules."

Mager's *Preparing Instructional Objectives* is an excellent small text for faculty members who need assistance in formulating course objectives.

4. Course Calendar

The calendar provides the relevant dates for assigned course topics, lectures, readings, projects, exams, etc. If the instructor changes the calendar during the course, new information should be supplied to students *in writing*.

5. Course Requirements

This section delineates exactly what students are expected to do in the course, on which they will be evaluated. Will homework count as part of the grade? How about attendance? Class participation? The course requirements spell out the instructor's (or the department's) position on these and any other issues relevant to the evaluation process. How much will each exam count? What about quizzes? Will any quiz grades be dropped? Will the students be expected to keep a journal? If so, will the instructor "evaluate" it and count it as a part of the course grade, and if so, how much? Specificity helps students.

6. Texts and Other Materials

Here, the instructor lists the texts and other materials required and/or recommended for the course. Which ones are on reserve at the library? For sale at the bookstore? Provided by the instructor as handouts?

7. Course Grading

Students read this section eagerly, for it spells out the procedures for evaluating achievement. Instructors should indicate what percentage of the course grade they will assign to each course activity (examinations, reports, term papers, homework, class participation, attendance, lab work, journal, etc.) Students have a right to know the relative importance of course requirements; knowing them at the beginning of the course helps them better budget their time.

8. Caveat

Since the course syllabus becomes a written legal covenant between the instructor and students in the course, each syllabus should end with a caveat of the following sort: "The above schedule and procedures in this course are subject to change in the event of extenuating circumstances." This caveat protects the instructor and department if changes in the syllabus need to be made once the course is underway.

Some faculty members will read this prescription for a course syllabus with disgust, concluding that such a detailed document will "take all the spontaneity and humanity" out of teaching. Nothing could be more inaccurate. A detailed syllabus encourages and facilitates student success. It does this by sharing some of the "secrets of learning," which our best and brightest students have always been able to grasp intuitively.

When "what the teacher wants" is shared with all the students, far more will succeed in the course. As Sharon Rubin wrote in a *Chronicle of Higher Education* "Point of View" (Aug. 7, 1985), "The syllabus is a small place to start bringing students and faculty members back together .... If students could be persuaded that we are really interested in their understanding of the material we offer, that we support their efforts to master it, and that we take their intellectual struggles seriously, they might respond by becoming more involved in our courses, by trying to live up to our expectations, and by appreciating our concern. Then the real work of learning can begin."

When we view a syllabus not merely as a brief outline of course dates and topics, but rather as a guide to shaping student learning in accordance with the teacher's expectations, the syllabus takes on considerably greater value. Its creation as a classroom document merits our highest efforts. And it deserves to be examined in faculty personnel decisions as evidence of a faculty member's commitment to and skills in teaching.

The Textbook Selection Checklist

Developed by Brian Hemmings and David Battersby

Ed.'s Note: How do we select textbooks? Generally we take a look at a number of available ones, maybe talk with some other instructors to find out what they use, and then try to find one that "marries" well with what we plan to teach in the course. In other words, we don't use clear-cut criteria. We don't submit potential texts to a systematic and organized review. We certainly don't consider texts in light of what research has discovered as to how students best learn from printed text. That is why we have chosen to include the only text selection checklist that we have seen which incorporates these concerns.

Please circle the appropriate response.

I. Coping with difficult words/concepts

1. Is italic or bold type used?	Yes/No
2. Are new concepts listed or defined?	Yes/No
3. Does a glossary appear within the textbook?	Yes/No
4. If yes, is it a 'running glossary' found in the margin?	Yes/No
5. Are footnotes avoided?	Yes/No

II. The use of instructional aids

6. Does an overview or summary precede each chapter?	Yes/No
7. Is there a summary at the end of each chapter?	Yes/No
8. Is there an advance organizer used at the beginning of the chapter?	Yes/No
9. If yes, does it provide a useful framework that helps clarify the ideas ahead?	Yes/No
10. Are behavioral objectives available for use?	Yes/No
11. Are additional questions inserted into the text?	Yes/No
12. If yes, do they adequately alert readers as to what information follows?	Yes/No
13. Does the author, by the use of instructional aids, indicate to the reader what material is important?	Yes/No

III. Typographical organization

14. Are the headings level and consistent within the chapters?	Yes/No
15. Do major headings appear in lower case?	Yes/No
16. Are subheadings written in the form of a question?	Yes/No
17. Are spatial cues effective for scanning?	Yes/No
18. Do chapters provide cues which are simple and clear to follow?	Yes/No
19. Is the text 'chunked' to promote more efficient reading?	Yes/No

IV. Presentation and appropriateness of illustrative materials

20. Are the illustrations used (i.e., pictures, diagrams, cartoons and photographs) relevant to the text?	Yes/No
21. Do the illustrations help to explain the text?	Yes/No
22. Do the illustrations provide crucial information for understanding the text?	Yes/No
23. Does the illustrative material have captions that are clear and relatively self-explanatory?	Yes/No
24. Is illustrative material positioned nearby to the text reference?	Yes/No
25. If yes, is it referenced clearly?	Yes/No

26. Does the author use a variety of materials (including flow charts, algorithms and information mapping) to maintain appeal?   Yes/No

27. If yes, are clear instructions given as to how to use these illustrative aids?   Yes/No

V. Provision for self-testing

28. Are questions provided at the end of each chapter to test understanding?   Yes/No

29. Is the questioning aimed at an appropriate level?   Yes/No

30. Are there answers available for the reader's use?   Yes/No

31. If yes, is information available which pinpoints the answers within the text, e.g., paragraph 3/page 67?   Yes/No

VI. Follow-up

32. Does the author provide additional notes and/or suggestions for further reading at the end of each chapter?   Yes/No

33. If yes, does the author discuss the relevance of the reference?   Yes/No

34. Are the follow-up materials appropriate for introductory students?   Yes/No

VII. Clarity of the author's intent

35. Does the author suggest to the reader how the textbook should be read?   Yes/No

36. If yes, does the author provide different instructions for beginning students and more advanced readers?   Yes/No

37. Do the intentions of the author 'link together' well?   Yes/No

38. If yes, do the cues provided by headings/subheadings assist in making the text more cohesive?   Yes/No

39. Is there a logic and a consistency in the page and chapter design?   Yes/No

40. Would the majority of readers find the reading required easy?   Yes/No

Checklist Score. Total the number of Yes responses.
Maximum Score = 40.

Blackboards and Overheads

Maryellen Weimer

Most instructors supplement their verbal presentation with visual reinforcements. They highlight important points, elaborate complex concepts or demonstrate applications most commonly by writing some or all of them on a blackboard or overhead transparency. These simple, straightforward instructional aids are easy to use, but their potential effectiveness is increased if you bear in mind the advice offered here.

The Blackboard

Technology marches on, but the blackboard (or greenboard or brownboard, depending on your classroom) remains the most easily accessible and commonly used visual aid for most professors. How well is it used? Well, let's just say that in most classrooms on at least some occasions it could be used more effectively. A handbook, *Teaching at Stanford*, offers these suggestions, some of which we have elaborated.

- Begin class with a clear blackboard. Notations from the previous class are distracting.

- Plan ahead. Figure out what areas of the blackboard are most clearly visible to the class. Try out different seats to see.

- Practice writing on the board. By consistently trying, most blackboard penmanship can be made large and legible.

- When writing on the board, avoid talking. It distracts the instructor, confuses the students, is hard to hear, and in most gatherings is considered rude because it forces one to speak without facing the audience.

- Do not stand in front of what you've just written.

- Use blackboard space systematically. When the space is full, erase — preferably the whole board, at least a substantial section.

- At the end of class, go to the back of the room and take a critical look at the board. Can't read it? Trouble. Can't see how one item relates to what surrounds it? Trouble. Can't figure out why something does or does not appear there? Trouble. If the boardwork doesn't make good sense to the instructor, there's an awfully good chance that students have been confused by it as well.

- After class, erase the board.

The Overhead Transparency

Using overhead transparencies? If you are, we'd like to offer some suggestions for using them more effectively. If you aren't, we think you ought to consider the potential of this instructional media aid.

Present material on overhead transparencies and you get these benefits:

- Using overhead projectors permits you to face the students when presenting written material.

- The projector is usually placed somewhere in the first or second row of students, providing you a perfect excuse for being in their space. That makes for better eye contact and conveys the less formal, more interactive teaching stance, especially desirable in large classes.

- Transparencies can (indeed should) be constructed before class, thereby encouraging a legible, organized display of the content.

- Transparencies make it easier to cover the content more efficiently, especially if diagrams and other visual materials, like charts and graphs, are also distributed to students. Neither teacher nor student now uses valuable class time reconstructing complicated drawings. Instead, they spend time filling in details.

- Intermittent use of transparencies, especially visually impressive ones, adds variety and interest as well as making the content more memorable.

- Transparencies keep well. They need not be reconstructed every time the course is taught, but can be part of a growing collection of instructional supplements.

As for using transparencies effectively, try these suggestions, adapted from *Instructional Media and the New Technologies of Instruction* by R. Heinich, M. Molanda, and J. Russell, 1985:

- Point to specific portions using a pencil or pointer. Lay the pencil directly on the transparency, because any elevation can put the pencil out of focus and any slight hand movement will be greatly exaggerated on the screen. Avoid pointing to the screen. To do this, one must typically stand in front of the projector, thereby needing to squint into its bright light and running the risk of having print or diagrams reflected on one's clothes and face — rarely becoming.

- Reveal the information one line or section at a time, masking other portions with a sheet of paper or cardboard 'windows' over the transparency. This strategy can be used to control impact and audience attention.

- Overlay new information one step at a time. Build up a complex idea by superimposing transparencies one at a time. Up to four overlays can be used together successfully.

Meeting a Class for the First Time

Wilbert J. McKeachie

The first class meeting, like any other situation in which you are meeting a group of strangers who will affect your well-being, is at the same time exciting and anxiety-producing for both students and teacher. Some teachers handle their anxiety by postponing it, simply handing out the syllabus and leaving. This does not convey the idea that class time is valuable, nor does it capitalize on the fact that first day excitement can be constructive. If you have prepared, you're in good shape; the students will be pleased that the instruction is under control, and focusing on meeting the students' concerns can not only help you quell your own anxiety but also make the first class interesting and challenging.

Other things being equal, anxiety is less disruptive in situations where stimulus events are clear and unambiguous. When the students know what to expect they can direct their energy more productively. An important function of the first day's meeting in any class is to provide this structure, that is, to present the classroom situation clearly, so that the students will know from the date of this meeting what you are like and what you expect. They come to the first class wanting to know what the course is all about and what kind of person the teacher is. To this end, the following concrete suggestions are offered.

One point to keep in mind both the first day and throughout the term is that yours is not the students' only class. They come to you from classes in chemistry, music, English, physical education, or rushing from their dormitory beds or from parking lots. The first few minutes need to help this varied group shift their thoughts and feelings to you and your subject.

You can ease them into the course gradually or you can grab their attention by something dramatically different, but in either case you need to think consciously about how you set the stage to facilitate achieving the course objectives. Even before the class period begins you can communicate nonverbally by such things as arranging the seats in a circle and putting your name on the board, or chat with early arrivals about what class they have come from or anything else that would indicate your interest in them.

Breaking the Ice

You will probably want to use the first period for getting acquainted and establishing goals. You might begin by informally asking freshmen to raise their hands, then sophomores, juniors, seniors, or out-of-staters. This gives you some idea of the composition of the class and gets students started participating.

You might then ask all class members (including yourself) to introduce themselves, tell where they're from, mention their field of concentration, and answer any questions the group has. Or you can ask each student to get acquainted with the persons sitting on each side and then go around the class with each student introducing the next or each repeating the names of all those who have been introduced — a good device for promoting development of rapport and for helping you learn the names too.

Having established a degree or freedom of communication, the class can discuss the objectives of the course. It seems helpful to list these on the board as class members suggest them or react to your suggestions. After class record them so that the class may periodically refer to them and check progress. Note that these are only a first approximation that can be altered and rephrased as the class becomes aware of new needs during the course.

Problem Posting[1]

The technique of posting problems is not only a useful icebreaker, but one of value whenever it is useful to stimulate interest and assist students in communicating their problems to one another. This may be the case not only at the beginning of the course, but also after a lecture or other classroom method has aroused anxiety or defensiveness. The technique may also be useful to you when you wish to avoid answering questions immediately yourself. This might be because you don't wish to establish an atmosphere in which you dominate, because you wish to lay more groundwork, or because you don't wish to reinforce or to engage in a colloquy with a particular questioner whose concerns are not likely to contribute toward achievement of the goals of the class as a whole.

Do these potentialities intrigue you? All you need do is to say something like, "Let's see if we can get all the questions out so that we can see what they are and how to handle them."

If it is the first class meeting, you might say, "Let's see what problems you'd like to have us tackle during the course. What sorts of concerns do you think that we might deal with?" or "What kinds of things have you heard about this course?"

The instructor's task then becomes that of understanding and recording briefly on the blackboard the problems contributed by the group. This means that you must be ready to accept all contributions, whether or not you yourself feel they are important. To test your understanding of the problem it may be useful to restate the problem in different words. Restatement may also be useful in removing emotional loading or in bringing out implicit feelings. When you feel that a question is ambiguous or too general, it is helpful to ask for an illustration or to ask other group members to help you understand.

As contributions begin to slow down, suggest stopping. But, if possible, the posting should not be ended before there has been a good pause, since some of the most deeply felt problems will not come out until the students have seen that the teacher is really accepting and noncritical. This is a point where sensitivity is particularly important, for one can often see the visible signs of conflict about whether or not to raise an emotion-laden problem. If such a problem does come out and elicits a new batch of problems, forget about the suggested ending and get the problems out.

It is important in problem posting to maintain an accepting, nonevaluative atmosphere. Thus, if other members of the group argue that someone's contribution is not really a problem or that the real problem is different from that stated, the teacher needs to make it clear that even though not everyone agrees about a given problem, anything that is a problem for any member of the group is entitled to be listed. Disagreement should be used to get additional problems out, rather than to persuade a group member to withdraw his contribution.

Inevitably some discussion will come out about solutions. While this should not be abruptly censored, if it becomes involved or lengthy the teacher may point out that the task of dealing with the problems comes later.

By the end of the problem posting the class normally has become better acquainted, has become used to active participation, has taken the first step toward developing an attitude of attempting to understand rather than compete with one another, has reduced the attitude that everything must come from the teacher, has learned that the teacher can listen as well as talk (and is not going to reject ideas different from his or her own), and, I hope, has begun to feel some responsibility for solving its own problems rather than waiting for them to be answered by the instructor.

From problem posting it is a natural transition to an introduction of ways to tackle the problems. The instructor here faces a dilemma. You need to give students some notion of what to expect. You need to give them a sense that you have worked to prepare for the course and will continue to work to help them learn, but you also want to leave students with a sense of their own responsibility for achieving course goals. Thus, in presenting a course outline, a summary of your evaluation and grading plans and other aspects of the course structure, you need to communicate their relevance to the problems raised by the students, your responsiveness to them, and a sense of willingness to change as the course develops.

Ambiguity may excite some students, but for most it simply arouses anxiety. A simple way to reduce some of that anxiety is to distribute a mimeographed course schedule.

Introducing the Teacher

In presenting the course outline and mechanics you also give the students some notion of the kind of person that you are. Although I am not recommending a complete personality change without benefit of at least short-term psychotherapy, three characteristics seem to be especially appreciated by the student:

- enthusiasm and willingness to work to make the course worthwhile,

- objectivity (the students will call it "fairness"),

- a sympathetic attitude toward the problems of the students.

If these characteristics apply to you at all, or if you think they do, let the students know it.

Presenting a syllabus is one demonstration that you have made an investment in the course. Obviously you want to be open to student input, but in my experience students resent much more than an authoritarian teacher the teacher who says, "This is your class," and leaves completely to the student the organization and structure of the course. Student-centered discussion is an effective teaching method, but students often interpret a student-centered beginning as evidence that the instructor is lazy and uninterested in the course.

Promoting the notion that you are objective or fair can best be handled in connection with marks and the assignment of grades. Remember that a large part of the students' motivation in the classroom situation is (perhaps unfortunately) directed toward the grades they hope to get from the course. The very least that students can expect of you is that this mark will be arrived at on some impartial basis.

The simplest way to show students that you are objective and fair is to let the students know that you are willing to meet and advise them. Indicate your office hours. In addition to this, students appreciate it if you are willing (and have the time) to spend a few minutes in the classroom after each class answering specific questions. Such queries most often concern questions of fact that can be answered briefly and would hardly warrant a trip to your office at a later time in another building, even if the student could be counted on to remember the question for that long. If your time permits, adjournment to a convenient snack bar or lounge may give students with special interests a chance to pursue them and get to know you better.

The first class is not the time to make sure the students understand your inadequacies and limitations. Frankly admitting that you don't know something is fine after the course is under way, but apologies in advance for lack of experience or expertise simply increase student insecurity.

Introducing the Textbook

To continue with the discussion of the first meeting of the class, we turn now to the presentation of the textbook(s). Here the most serious question that arises concerns possible disagreement between the textbook and the materials you intend to present in your lectures. Unfortunately this is a matter that cannot always be solved simply by judicious selection of text materials. In some cases, there is simply no book available that presents certain material as you would like to have it presented. In others, the textbook is decided upon by someone other than yourself, and you have to make the best of it.

In the case where disagreement is inevitable, the students have a right to know which version to accept as *truth* and what they are supposed to do about such discrepancies on examinations. By facing the situation squarely, you can not only escape from the horns of this dilemma, but also turn it to your advantage. Explain that rival interpretations stand or fall on the basis of pertinent evidence, and plan to give your reasons for disagreeing with the textbook This procedure will accomplish two things: 1) it will give the student the notion that your opinions are based upon evidence, and 2) it will frequently point up current problems in theory that often have great appeal for the serious student.

Avoid a tirade against the author. This may serve as an emotional catharsis for the instructor, but for the student, any severe criticism you raise may generalize to the textbook as a whole. Or, if the student is not convinced by your argument, it may generalize to much of what you have to say.

Questions

Even in a large lecture it seems well to interrupt these first descriptions of the course for questions. Some of the questions will be designed as much to test you as to get information. Often the underlying questions are such things as:

- "Are you rigid?"
- "Will you really try to help students?"
- "Are you easily rattled?"
- "Are you a person as well as a teacher?"
- "Can you handle criticism?"

In general, it is good to respond to the surface content and not to the indirect one in this first class before trust has been built up. Nevertheless, an awareness of the feelings behind the questions may help temper your responses.

Finally, ask students to take two minutes at the end of class, to write their reactions to the first day (anonymously). This accomplishes two things:

- It indicates your interest in learning from them and starts building a learning climate in which they have responsibilities for thinking about their learning and influencing your teaching.

- It gives you feedback, often revealing doubts or questions students were afraid to verbalize orally.

Notes

[1] This technique is one I learned from Norman R.F. Maier, described in his book *Problem-Solving Discussions and Conferences: Leadership Methods and Skills* (New York: McGraw-Hill, 1963).

SECTION 3

As You Teach for the First Time

The course is planned. You're ready to go. Now, what are you going to do in class? If you're going to be like most college teachers, you'll lecture. (Don't believe us? Check the figures in the opening paragraph of the Cashin piece.) We don't particularly advocate that, especially if that's all you plan to do, but our strongest hunch bets that, at least on occasion if not regularly, you'll "teach by the spoken word." Let's not quibble about how much time you'll devote to lecture (as opposed to discussion or some other instruction method). Let's define lecture broadly, as Cashin does, and recommend you attend to these materials on lecture even if you don't intend to spend much time at all in this kind of one-way communication.

The lecture has strengths; Cashin lists nine of them. It also has weaknesses; Cashin lists nine of them. But we don't think it's quite that balanced — maybe in theory, but not in practice. Many, many of the faculty members we've seen teach don't lecture particularly well. We think Cashin has identified the problem; we just think it's a lot more serious than he admits. "Lectures require an *effective speaker*. The lecturer must be loud enough to be heard; and also must vary pitch, tone of voice, and pace of delivery. Lecturers must be verbally fluent. These skills are not typically stressed in Ph.D. programs." (p. 60)

Cashin's list of effective speaking skills emphasizes the mechanical. Weaver sees the problem from a bit broader perspective: "It saddens me to report that most students are not sponges for knowledge. Students, it seems to me, are rather like wheelbarrows: they stand still unless pushed!" (p. 65) That being the case, to be effective, lecturers must do more than transfer information. They must make efforts to motivate and interest students — which does involve matters of voice, but it calls for an approach and attitude toward teaching, as illustrated by naturalist instructor Stewart and described to us by Stasz.

Teaching students, whether via the lecture, discussion or other methods, hinges on a number of key ingredients which we attempt to address in this section. Again our selection of issues reflects areas where we see faculty getting into trouble, places where lecturing (and sometimes discussion) often lets students down. Whether teaching courses designed by others or courses of their own design, faculty have lots of content to cover. Lecturing lets them cover it efficiently, albeit hurriedly. Students are easily left in the dust, which is why instructors must attend to matters of pace.

Faculty regularly complain that classes are getting larger. No one has much in the way of proof, but even if you've taught before, the differences between a class of 25 and 250 are sizeable. If your first teaching assignment includes a large class, you need survival equipment and supplies.

Humor and examples may seem like strange bedfellows, but both represent ways of enlivening instruction, ways of holding student attention and ways of making understanding easier. Both are double-edged swords as well. If the humor is at another's expense, hurts or hides feelings, using it can turn students against teachers. If students cannot relate to examples, if they inaccurately reflect what they are supposed to explain, if they are bland and boring, examples offer yet another reason for students to tune out.

Up to this point, we've been pretty plain about our feelings toward lectures. If you think we've been stressing the problems, you're right. Basically it boils down to this: most teachers spend entirely too much time talking. Students learn when they are actively involved, working with the material, responding and reacting to it. We think college teaching would be a whole lot better if it were a whole lot more interactive.

Why then do we only include two short readings on participation and discussion? Because we've assembled a book of readings like this one on that topic and would like to encourage you to take a look at it. *Classroom Communication: Collected Readings for Effective Discussion and Questioning* is available from the publisher of this companion volume.

Classroom interaction helps to make passive students active; so does the group-inquiry technique Kraft proposes. He writes of his experience, "It took me 13 years of student and classroom experiments to develop this form of group-inquiry. It came out of the conviction that students did not grow and develop, did not genuinely learn, with traditional teacher-dominated practices. I now believe such practices are obsolete and must be abandoned in favor of something like group-inquiry." (p. 99) This particular strategy may not work with your content, but it's still worth considering as an example of how teachers must explore and experiment with all sorts of innovative instructional practices if students are to learn.

You might want to read all of this section now, which is fine. It might be more valuable if you review the articles now and return to them for a more reflective read-through once you've actually started teaching. You can't learn to lecture, discuss or otherwise interact with students in "theory." The theory gives you ideas, but you will learn to teach by *teaching*, in class and most especially on one of those days in class when things don't go well. Return to these readings then. We selected them because they offer concrete, practical advice.

Improving Lectures

William E. Cashin

"Given the recent invention of the printing press, why do college professors continue to lecture so much?" —Anonymous

The question is not trivial. The lecture may be the most widely used teaching approach in U.S. higher education. Looking at data from 6307 classes that used IDEA in the late 1970s, 24% were listed as "Lecture," 27% as "Lecture and Discussion," and 20% as "Lecture with Lab."

There are faculty who are convinced that lecturing is the most appropriate teaching approach in almost every case. There are others who are equally convinced that lecturing is almost never appropriate. The position of this paper is that it is impossible to decide upon an effective teaching approach without first deciding upon your instructional goals. Lecturing is very appropriate for some goals, and very inappropriate for others.

Every reader undoubtedly has an idea of what is meant by a "lecture," and dictionary definitions do not shed much additional light: lecture — an exposition on a given subject delivered before an audience or class for the purpose of instruction, or a method of teaching by discourse as opposed to conversation or seminar. Etymologically, to lecture means to read. In the medieval universities the professor did read from his notes because those were the only "books" available.

Unless otherwise stated in this paper, "lecture" will focus on teaching by the spoken word with emphasis on one-way communication: the teacher talks, and (hopefully) the students listen, recognizing that most courses listed as lecture in college catalogs involve some two-way communication, question and answer and the like — a practice we heartily approve.

Strengths of the Lecture Approach

The obvious answer to the question of why we continue to lecture so much is that lecturing continues to be useful in achieving a number of instructional goals. Walker and McKeachie (1967) argue that the lecture approach has two unique strengths: it can communicate the intrinsic interest of the subject matter, and it can present the newest developments. Other authors have listed other goals which, although they may not be unique to lecturing, are well served by that approach.

1. Lectures can communicate the *intrinsic interest* of the subject matter. Like live theatre, lectures can convey the speaker's enthusiasm in a way that no book or other media can. Enthusiasm stimulates interest and interested, stimulated people tend to learn more.

2. Lectures can cover *material not otherwise available*. This includes original research or recent developments which may only be available from papers or articles not yet included in textbooks.

3. Lectures can *organize material in a special way*. Lectures may be a faster, simpler method of presenting materials fitted to the needs or interests of a particular audience.

4. Lectures can convey *large amounts of information*. Lectures are probably most often used to cover facts, generalizations, and the like. This was the original purpose of the lecture before the invention of the printing press. Lectures continue to be useful to convey information that is not available in print. When the material is otherwise available, e.g., in textbooks or programmed texts, you should consider whether lecturing on the material is desirable. It very well may be if, for example, the students are not motivated enough to study the material on their own, or they lack the required reading skills.

5. Lectures can communicate to *many listeners* at the same time. With the proper audiovisual support, a skilled lecturer can communicate effectively with a few hundred (or even a few thousand) listeners. (Unskilled lecturers should not try to lecture to groups of any size.)

6. Lecturers can *model* how professionals in a particular discipline approach a question or problem. This modeling behavior is one of the major characteristics of the instructor-centered teacher described by Axelrod (1976). The audience can watch firsthand as the lecturer "thinks" like professionals in the field.

7. Lectures permit *maximum teacher control*. From the teacher's point of view this can be an advantage. The instructor chooses what material to cover, and whether to answer questions.

8. Lectures present *minimum threat to the student*. Students are not required to do anything. From the students' point of view this may be an advantage.

9. Lectures emphasize *learning by listening*. This is an advantage for students who learn well this way, which may increasingly be the case for students raised on television viewing.

Weaknesses of the Lecture Approach

The lecture approach has a number of strengths; unfortunately, it also has a number of weaknesses. Both must be taken into consideration when you are deciding whether giving a lecture is appropriate for a particular part of your course.

1. Lectures *lack feedback* to the instructor about the students' learning: "... in the long run, it is what the learner does rather than what the teacher does that really counts in teaching" (Dressel and Marcus, 1982, p. xix.). The major drawback of a strict lecture approach is that it does not provide the lecturer with any systematic information about whether and what the students are learning or not learning. Granted, there are a lot of nonverbal cues available if you look around.

2. In lectures, the *students are passive*; at least they are more passive than the lecturer. The more active the learner, the more learning is likely to take place.

3. Students' *attention wanes quickly*, in 15 or 25 minutes according to studies (Bligh, 1972).

4. Information learned in lectures tends to be *forgotten quickly*. This general statement depends considerably on how passive the students are. Students who simply listen to a lecture will tend to forget the material more quickly than students who listen and take notes, who in turn will remember less than students who take notes and are involved in some kind of question/answer session, etc. The more active the student, and the more senses involved in the learning, the more he or she is likely to remember more material, and for a longer time.

5. Lectures presume that all students are learning at the *same pace and level of understanding*. Of course, this is hardly ever true. Unlike written passages that can be reread or tapes that can be rewound, lectures proceed at a pace determined by the lecturer, not the individual student.

6. Lectures are *not well suited to higher levels of learning*: application, analysis, synthesis, influencing attitudes or values, developing motor skills. Lecturing is best suited to the lower levels of knowledge and understanding. If you want students to think critically or to write well, you need to do something other than lecture.

7. Lectures are *not well-suited to complex, detailed, or abstract material*. The more difficult the material becomes, the more individual differences among the students are going to influence the pace and level of the students' learning. Therefore, self-paced and/or two-way communication teaching approaches become preferable to lecturing.

8. Lectures require an *effective speaker*. The lecturer must be loud enough to be heard, and also must vary pitch, tone of voice, and pace of delivery. Lecturers must be verbally fluent. These skills are not typically stressed in Ph.D. programs, the terminal degree for college teachers.

9. Lectures emphasize *learning by listening*, which is a disadvantage for students who prefer to learn by reading, or by doing, or some other mode.

Recommendations

This part attempts to summarize the recommendations about improving lectures made by several of the authors listed in the Further Readings section at the end of this paper. Citations will only be given where a specific author has something to recommend not included by other authors.

Preparation and Organization

These recommendations concern what should be done when the lecture is being planned, before you enter the classroom.

1. *Fit the lecture to your audience.* Try to make the lecture relevant to your audience and, therefore, more interesting. This means that you will have to gather some information about your listeners beforehand.

2. *Select your topic.* You will never be able to cover everything. Selecting your topic will determine the focus of your lecture and provide a context within which you make other decisions.

3. *Prepare an outline.* Some people suggest five to nine major points. If you attempt to cover too much, your audience will actually learn, and also remember, less. The object of a lecture is not just to cover the material, but to have the listeners learn.

4. *Organize your points.* This can be done in a number of ways: for example, chronologically, causally, in ascending or descending order, spatially, or by presenting a problem and then possible solutions. (See Day, 1980, for some alternative ways to organize your lecture notes.)

5. *Decide upon minor points,* or the points you wish to include under each major point.

6. *Select examples.* Almost all writers agree that illustrations, etc., help people both to understand and to remember.

7. *Present more than one side of an issue.* You must do this if you wish to convince your listeners of the validity of a given position — if that is one of your purposes — unless your audience is completely naive and incapable of thinking of any counterarguments. You should do it simply to help them understand various implications of an issue.

Presentation and Clarity

This section and the next concern two different aspects of lecturing while you are actually in the classroom.

8. *Speak clearly and loud enough to be heard.* It seems obvious, but I suspect that we have all sinned against this prescription. Perhaps in the very first class you should suggest that people signal you if they cannot hear, e.g., cup a hand behind their ear.

9. *Avoid distracting mannerisms,* verbal tics like "ah" or "you know," straightening your notes or tie or beads.

10. *Provide an introduction.* Begin with a concise statement, something that will preview the lecture. Give the listeners a set or frame of reference for the remainder of your presentation. Refer to previous lectures. Attract and focus their attention.

11. *Present an outline.* Write it on the chalkboard, or use an overhead transparency or a handout. Then be sure that you refer to it as you move from point to point in your lecture.

12. *Emphasize principles and generalizations.* Research suggests that these are what people really remember — and they are probably what you really want to teach.

13. *Repeat your points* in two or three different ways. Your listeners may not have heard it the first time, or understood it, or had time to write it down. Include examples or concrete ideas. These help both understanding and remembering. Use short sentences.

14. *Stress important points.* This can be done by how you say it. It can also be done explicitly, e.g., "Write this down," "This is important," "This will be on the test." If you are modeling thinking, point out the thought processes as you go along.

15. *Pause.* Give your listeners time to think and to write.

Stimulation and Interest

The previous section made some recommendations that dealt with cognitive aspects of your classroom presentation; this section deals with affective aspects.

16. *Use effective speech techniques.* Talk — do not read your lecture. Vary your inflection, gestures, position, pace of lecture, etc.

17. *Be enthusiastic.* If you do not think the material is worth learning, why should the students? If you do think so, communicate that.

18. *Start with a question, problem, or controversy.* Very early in the lecture you need something that will catch the listeners' attention, something to stir their interest. There is nothing wrong with being dramatic as long as you also have content. No matter how profound your content, the students won't learn anything from you if they are half asleep.

19. *Be relevant.* Use materials and examples that the students can relate to, things from their previous learning or experience, things from "real life."

20. *Use AV.* Models, films, recordings, etc. make a lecture more vivid and immediate; they also provide variety. Demonstrations and experiments serve the same purpose.

21. *Use humor*. Almost every writer agrees that a certain amount of humor or personal anecdotes enhances a lecture. There are two cautions:

- The humor should not be at the expense of the students or offend the reasonable sensibilities of any group.

- Avoid ego trips.

22. *Provide change*. Research suggests that most people's attention wanes after 15-25 minutes. I suggest that you introduce some kind of change about every 15 minutes. This does not mean ending your lecturing. It could simply be stopping for questions, or putting a transparency on the overhead, or moving to a different part of the room — but do something different.

Feedback and Interaction

Strictly speaking this is not part of a lecture defined as "one-way communication." But none of the writers recommend that kind of lecture and very, very few college lecture courses are that restricted.

23. *Look at your listeners*. Most audiences provide a multitude of nonverbal clues about whether they are paying attention, whether they understand, and whether they agree.

24. *Solicit questions*. Even if all you do is occasionally pause, look around, and ask if there are any questions, you will have significantly added to the effectiveness of your lecture. It will give you some feedback from the students.

25. *Use discussion techniques*. There are a number of group techniques that can be used, even with hundreds of listeners, to increase their involvement. Several years ago some institutions had large lecture halls wired so that the instructor could put a multiple-choice question on the screen and the students could punch in their answers. The same thing can be accomplished by giving the students sets of five different colored index cards to hold up for their answers: red for option 1, yellow for 2, etc. You can call on a student who chose the correct answer (color) and have him or her explain why; or call on a student who chose an alternative that contained a common misconception. Interactions like this achieve two things:

- They actively involve the students' thinking about the material.

- They give you feedback about what the students are learning.

26. *Use praise*. In your give-and-take with students, make positive comments when they are warranted; doing so increases learning.

27. *Use a lecture committee*. This is something McKeachie (1978) uses in large general psychology classes. Basically, it is a committee of students which meets with the instructor periodically to provide student feedback about how the course is progressing and to react to ideas for future classes.

Conclusion

This paper has attempted to summarize much of what has been written about improving lecturing. Readers should be aware that, although there are empirical data supporting some of the recommendations made in this paper, most of the research is such that it would *not* compel belief. No case is being made that you *must* do these things to lecture effectively. Rather, these are some suggestions you might consider. If they are of help, fine; if not, try something else.

Lecturing is appropriate for many of the instructional goals of college-level classes. Lecturing is a craft, that is, a learnable skill. These suggestions will not ensure greatness, but for about 99% of us, they are steps in the right direction.

References

Axelrod, J. *The University Teacher as Artist*. San Francisco: Jossey-Bass, 1976.

Bligh, D.A. *What's the Use of Lectures?* 3rd ed. Harmondsworth, Middlesex, England: Penguin Books, 1972.

Day, R.S. "Teaching from Notes: Some Cognitive Consequences." In W. J. McKeachie, ed., *Learning, Cognition, and College Teaching*. New Directions for Teaching and Learning, No. 2. San Francisco: Jossey-Bass, 1980. Pp. 95-112.

Dressel, P.L., & Marcus, D. *On Teaching and Learning in College*. San Francisco: Jossey-Bass, 1982.

McKeachie, W.J. *Teaching Tips: A Guidebook for the Beginning Teacher*. 7th ed. Lexington, MA: D.C. Heath, 1978. Pp. 22-34.

Walker, E.L., & McKeachie, W.J. *Some Thoughts about Teaching the Beginning Course in Psychology*. Belmont: CA: Brooks/Cole Publishing, 1976.

Further Readings

All of the readings included in this list are recommended. However, as a help to the reader, there are two asterisks following the reading recommended as first choice, and one for second choices.

Bligh, D.; Ebrahim, G.J.; Jacques, D.; & Piper, D.W. *Teaching Students*. Devon, England: Exeter University Teaching Services, 1975. Pp. 101-108.

Brock, S.C. *Aspects of Lecturing*. Manhattan, KS: Kansas State University. Center for Faculty Evaluation and Development, 1977. 17 pp.

Cashin, W.E.; Brock, S.D.; & Owens, R.E. *Answering and Asking Questions*. Manhattan, KS: Kansas State University. Center for Faculty Evaluation and Development, 1976. 17 pp.

Davis, R.H., & Alexander, L.T. *The Lecture Method: Guides for the Improvement of Instruction in Higher Education*, No. 5. East Lansing: Michigan State University, 1977. 18 pp.

Day, R.S. "Teaching from Notes: Some Cognitive Consequences." In W. J. McKeachie, ed., *Learning, Cognition, and College Teaching: New Directions for Teaching and Learning*, No. 2. San Francisco: Jossey-Bass, 1980. Pp. 95-112. *

Eble, K.E. *The Craft of Teaching*. San Francisco: Jossey-Bass, 1976. Pp. 42-53. **

Fuhrmann, B.S., & Grasha, A.F. *A Practical Handbook for College Teachers*. Boston: Little, Brown, 1983. Pp. 52-63.

Hyman, R.T. *Ways of Teaching*. 2nd ed. Philadelphia: J.B. Lippincott, 1974. Pp. 208-230.

Lowman, J. *Mastering the Techniques of Teaching*. San Francisco: Jossey-Bass, 1984. Pp. 96-118.

McKeachie, W.J. *Teaching Tips: A Guidebook for the Beginning Teacher*. 7th ed. Lexington, MA: D.C. Heath, 1978. Pp. 22-34. *

Effective Lecturing Techniques: Alternatives to Classroom Boredom

Richard L. Weaver II

Plato sometimes had Aristotle as his only listener to lectures which he delivered in Athens. When this was the case, he merely proceeded with his lecture as usual, remarking that when he had Aristotle for a hearer he had the better half of Athens. On the same principle, when you get up to lecture before a class, you too may have only one listener (excluding yourself) — the student who really wants to listen to what you have to say. Some students will be absent, some will not care, some will simply want the notes. Lecturing is difficult. This is partly because of student apathy, brought about by the instructors' negative attitudes of sustaining interest. Also, it is partly because the stereotypes surrounding "the lecture" are themselves negative.

Rather than lecturing the reader on lecturing, it might be more advantageous if I could ask each reader — individually — what is it you *really* want? That is the key. When you *really* want something badly enough, you will go after it with a passion. And you will probably get it. That may be precisely what is missing from education today. *Passion.* How many teachers did you have during your entire educational career who really cared? I mean *really* cared? It is probably something I should not admit, but after eight years of formal education at two of our "outstanding" institutions — the University of Michigan and Indiana University — I can count the number of really fantastic teachers I had on one hand and have three fingers left over. That is a crime! No, I think it is probably a lack of passion. The dictionary defines that as a lack of "intense, driving, or overmastering feeling." It also describes it as a lack of "strong liking for or devotion to some activity, object, or concept." But it is not the lack that will be the focus of this article; rather, it is the opposite.

So, what is it that you *really* want? Do you want to be an inspirational teacher? Is this one of your goals as an educator? If so, let me suggest that you use the A.I.D.A. formula. It does not guarantee passion, but it is likely to take its user quite a distance from its opposite. "A" stands for *attention*; "I" is for *interest*; "D" for *desire*; and "A" for *action*. Each of these is crucial to success in lecturing.

Attention

It is too bad that things were not arranged so that an empty head, like an empty stomach, would not let its owner rest until he or she put something into it. If that were the case, I would not need to be writing about lecturing — students would be sponges for knowledge. They would hang on the instructor's every word. It saddens me to report that most students are not sponges for knowledge. Students, it seems to me, are rather like wheelbarrows: they stand still unless pushed!

The lecturer's first job must be to reach out and grasp student attention. Let me offer several ideas on capturing attention:

1. Before beginning a lecture, allow a couple of minutes of "adjustment" time — letting the students get wound down, reoriented, and set. If you put your key sentence first, they are likely to miss it. I often start a lecture with some nonsensical item just to let them know that I am starting to talk: "This lecture is like all my other lectures," I might say. "It starts out slowly, then tapers off."

2. Try to get students to see where you are going, what you are going to do with the time, and how what you are going to do relates or eventually will relate to them. You can do this by giving some "initial partition" — a forecast or brief review of major points or ideas to be covered in the lecture. Then, if transitions are weak or nonexistent, or if students miss one of them, they can still follow the lecture.

3. If you can begin with a story, an example, a startling statistic, a personal experience, or something that has significant attention-holding appeal, that will help capture attention. Sometimes it helps to know that that's the kind of material one should be looking for to begin a lecture.

But in all of this, too, it is important to know that attention does not last long. It is fleeting. Thus, you do not want to think about holding attention just at the outset of the lecture; holding attention is important throughout the lecture. You hold attention throughout a lecture by using some of the parts of the formula — for example, interest.

Interest

The real, uncoerced zest for learning goes out of education when it is reduced to a routine transmittal of pre-digested information — and, unfortunately, that is what most lecturing amounts to: *a routine transmittal of pre-digested information.* That is not, very clearly, what holds student attention or gets them excited about education or learning.

What can you do to hold student interest? There are several things that are very effective:

1. Adapt your lecture material to your audience. Share information with them that concerns them. Share information with them that they can handle. Try not to get needlessly esoteric or theoretical if the students cannot handle it or if the material does not merit it. Analyze your audience first to find out where they are.

2. Do not try to pack your whole educational career — all that you have learned — into the course or lecture. For example, in an Advanced Public Speaking course I taught my first year out of graduate school, more than 50 students passed through my classroom — 25 on the first day. I ended up teaching a seminar of five students. My approach, my syllabus, and my expectations were way out of line with student expectations or desires. I simply wanted my students to know all that I had learned.

3. It is better to cover a few points or topics in depth than many points or topics superficially. Narrowing the focus will help hold students' interest. Remember, too, they can only remember so much.

4. Interest also comes from variety: variety (a) in kinds of information shared, and variety (b) in format.

a. Most speakers know that a long string of statistics, a series of historical anecdotes, or a long list of facts does not hold attention well. Variety of material captures attention. As a lecturer, try to assemble facts as well as examples, opinions as well as illustrations, statistics as well as anecdotes. Even a good storyteller can bore an audience if his or her repertoire includes just one story after another, with no other variety.

I suspect that real learning probably occurs more in the form of spontaneous combustion than as a response to methodical coercion. Capitalize, if you can, on ideas that are generated at the moment — products of that particular, unique circumstance. You probably heard about the professor who said, "I shall now attempt to explain what I have in mind" — and then began to read his carefully prepared notes. That is when a lecture can be defined as "a process by which the notes of the professor become the notes of the student, without passing through the minds of either."

b. Variety also results from format. You must vary your lecturing format:

- Do not just talk at students. Try to incorporate questions as well. Strive for give-and-take wherever possible.

- Move around. Do not stand in one place. It is a stereotype that "lecture" means that the lecturer and the lectern become fused together as one.

- Use visual aids — the blackboard, charts, graphs, maps, pictures, books, magazines. One student summarized it well when she said, "I'd rather *see* a lecture than *hear* one."

- Use films, slides, the overhead projector, or television. In my ten-lecture series in a basic-communication course, I use television once, audio tapes twice, music once, the overhead projector sometimes and over 900 slides. In two lectures I use three slide projectors at the same time.

- In addition to adapting your material to your audience, trying not to pack everything you have learned into your lecture, narrowing your focus to a few key points, and using a variety of information and variety in format, remember that interest also comes from the use of humor.

From what does humor come? What does the use of humor mean? Using humor does not necessarily mean trying to get the big guffaw. Rather, it is the instructor's willingness to laugh at himself or herself or at life. It should not be forced. To force a sense of humor can be worse than revealing none at all. The best kind of humor is that which grows or develops naturally from a situation. Thus, to enhance one's use of humor, one should try to develop a sense of spontaneity — to be able to play off any situation that might develop in a flexible, natural and comfortable manner.

Students learn best in an environment where they are not only comfortable, but where they enjoy the situation. Enjoyment can be encouraged through the use of humor. It is contagious; thus, if the teacher enjoys what he or she is doing, it is more likely that students will also enjoy the situation.

The word "lecture" has come to have a negative connotation in the minds of many — even in the minds of those who have to prepare them. This is because:

- educators feel students do not achieve as well in this situation,

- students are apathetic toward lectures,

- it is difficult to sustain interest using this format,

- one must constantly revise and update lecture material, and

- there is little interaction in lectures.

To counter some of these negative characteristics, it may help if you view the lecture as a speech. There is no reason that a lecture must be monotonous and dull, delivered from manuscript, or devoid of personality. The lecture that will live in the minds of students long after it is presented (to say nothing of the lecturer, remembered for stirring the mind), is the one prepared for as carefully and thoughtfully as for a speech. The same amounts of time and energy must be given; the same amounts of vivid and illustrative material must be included. And the same amount of desire must accompany both.

Desire

Desire is a key element — as noted at the outset of this article. Without desire, nothing else matters. That is why I asked the question in the beginning: "Do you want to be an inspirational teacher?" If not, you probably will not be!

Enthusiasm is the most convincing orator. It is like the infallible law of nature. The simplest person, fired with enthusiasm, is more persuasive than the most eloquent person without it. Enthusiasm is the lubricant that oils the machinery of action. But — unfortunately, you know as well as I that it is much easier to handle the tools than it is to light the spark!

There is no question, however, that those lecturers who demonstrate dynamism in their presentations have less difficulty holding attention. You need a certain amount of aggressiveness, boldness and forcefulness. You can do this by:

1. demonstrating an active commitment to the topic. You have to show what you have done, how you are involved, and what your plans are for future involvement. Active commitment!

2. demonstrating an emotional commitment — complete ego involvement. Let your audience know that you believe in what you are doing, that your knowledge, your ideas, and your information can make a difference. Be a believer!

3. being intellectually and physically powerful — try to eliminate speech hesitancies such as "uh," "er," "you know," "I mean," and "OK." Be a powerful speaker!

As I said, enthusiasm is the lubricant that oils the machinery of action. Attention, interest and desire can be revealed through the lecturer's action.

Action

Demosthenes (the famous Greek orator) was once asked, "What are the most important parts of the speech?" He replied, "Action, action, action." Because he was an effective orator, we should heed his words.

Action means variety, change and activity. It also means bodily action. Your concern, your belief, and your commitment as an educator, will probably be revealed to your students more as a result of your nonverbal behavior than as a result of what you say. What you have to do is try to control your nonverbal communication so that it has a positive effect. What can you do?

1. Be prompt, efficient, prepared, organized and alert. These are nonverbal features that arouse in the student feelings of: "This person really cares" — or "This person cares less. Why should I?"

2. In your presentation, maintain eye contact with the students. Show them that they matter — that their presence in front of you makes a difference. When you maintain eye contact with them, you put them in the spotlight — then they bask in the warmth of its glow.

3. Maintain an alert and erect posture. Have you ever watched the way people walk? You can tell the importance of their mission by how they hold themselves. Show your students that your mission is important.

4. Move about in front of the class with certainty and surety. Try to eliminate random, casual or distracting movement.

5. Gesture comfortably and naturally. Do not plan your gestures, but plan to gesture. It reveals activity and interest.

6. Be spontaneous, poised and at ease. Reveal that you are flexible and willing to adapt to anything that occurs.

As a concerned large-group lecturer, I wanted to know whether or not I was fulfilling the expectations of my students — almost 3,000 per year. So, in an initial survey, I asked a group of them (close to 400) to list, in an open-ended way, those characteristics they considered to be most important in a large-group lecturer. This was before they even got to know me. Then, I took those items that received the most responses — 15 of them — and I asked another group of students (close to 300) to rank-order them.

A large-group lecturer should, the students — undergraduates — said:

1. know the topic well and explain it clearly

2. give a well-organized presentation

3. capture and hold attention

4. have interesting lecture material

5. be competent in the field

6. be enthusiastic

You will note that these characteristics do fit into the A.I.D.A. formula very comfortably.

The formula is not a miracle drug. But remembering it can help restore, or bring, a sense of passion to your teaching.

A — reach out there and grasp their *attention*

I — find materials and use approaches designed to hold their *interest*

D — reveal an honest *desire* to help students and to promote learning

A — allow your bodily *action* to reinforce and enhance your ideas

That is what passion in teaching is all about.

Lecturing Is Not Dead — A Nature Hike Through Effective Teaching

Clarice Stasz

A little pedagogy is dangerous! Consider this scenario. Apart from scheduling a film or guest lecture, a teacher turns a class over to the students. They come to class each time to discuss the material or hear one another's presentations. In self-delusion the teacher points to research on the positive effects of active learning as proof he is doing a better job than the lecturer next door. When asked, students will claim to have "gotten something." The problem is, their learning will be idiosyncratic and unpredictable from one semester to the next. The teacher has failed to provide a system of understanding.

Research on active learning does not excuse the teacher to play recreation director. The danger in applying active learning blindly is that, done badly, it can look good. The class bubbles with the students "aware" and the teacher "approved." This makes it easy to trash lectures. After all, who among us has not experienced a sore coccyx listening to colleagues at professional meetings? Moreover, when we learn in everyday life, we learn by doing. But that doing is greatly facilitated when we encounter an expert who takes on the role of teacher. That happened to me when I explored birdwatching.

To the casual observer, bird hikes look alike — a group of people with binoculars following some guy who makes "pishing" sounds at the bushes. I'd been on many such hikes. It wasn't until I went out with Marin County naturalist Bob Stewart, though, that my competence began to grow. One trip with Bob was worth hours of hiking with others. After being with him I could make better use of my field guides and bird-call records. This made me reflect on what made him a teacher instead of a recreation director.

A teacher saves time by showing the best paths through difficult, fearful, and complex sets of information. A recreation director lets one backtrack and stick with what looks safe. While any walk with Bob seems spontaneous and casual, it is carefully planned. He does extensive hiking the day before to locate "hot spots." This means any trip is likely to have important discoveries.

Bob is alert to the need to pace the information and arrange for rest breaks at the right time. One always feels he is in charge. His outings have a predictable rhythm that frees me to attend to the birds, not worry about potential discomfort.

Bob also uses classic teaching techniques. Among them:

- *Modeling*, or talking aloud the thought processes he follows in making an identification.

- *Playing dumb*, so novices have time to figure out a bird.

- *Giving the wrong answer*, to see if people are just copying him or are alert to the process.

- *Organizing data*, by finding similar birds to compare and contrast.

- *Mnemonic guides*, so that even the tone-deaf can distinguish songs.

- *Testing*, by asking hikers to make identifications and explain reasoning.

- *Repeating* the same knowledge in various ways.

- *Building confidence* by acknowledging others' discoveries.

- *Diagnosing errors* by helping to figure out where the reasoning is off.

Of course, teaching is not the mere application of pedagogical techniques. Expertise matters. Bob is up-to-date and fully engaged in his field. He is modest about this role, and accepts it as a duty to stay informed. A teacher is a master who wants to make students peers. Bob seems to enjoy novices more on hikes than fellow experts. Novices ask the interesting questions.

The value of active learning is real. It cannot be denied. But those activities associated with it need to be under the firm direction of the teacher in charge. Otherwise those activities can be a waste of time: random walks — fun for all — but ultimately lost opportunities. However one teaches, one has to preserve that expert status because, at least on occasion, we expect an expert to tell us how it is.

How to Pace Your Lectures

Marilla Svinicki

The pace of your lectures was:

a. too fast

b. about right

c. too slow

And your class split evenly across the three choices, right? This article offers some ideas about pacing lectures: determining *how much* and *how fast*.

What influences perceived pace? The important word here is "perceived." The pace of a lecture really has little to do with how fast (measured in number of words per minute) a lecturer talks. Rather, what students mean by pace has a lot more to do with whether or not they can "listen" at the same speed. That is, can they follow what the lecturer is saying?

When considering the pace of a lecture, we should be looking at some of the following areas:

What are students supposed to be doing while you're talking?

What the listeners do while the lecture is going on strongly influences perception of pace. If they're supposed to be listening only, then words and ideas can come at a much faster rate and still be understood. If, on the other hand, they are supposed to take notes or do some thinking or problem-solving, the lecture must slow down accordingly.

And the type of notes they are taking affects the appropriateness of the rate even more. For example, exact notes on detailed information require a slower presentation rate than broad strokes on large concepts.

How much of the material is new?

The more new ideas contained in a lecture, the more rushed the pace will seem, simply because it takes longer to process new material than old. Old material engages the listener primarily in recognition tasks. As ideas are raised, they trigger already existing memory structures; no new structures need to be developed to accommodate them. The result: a lot of head-nodding — "Oh yes, I recognize that idea." And very little processing time is needed to deal with the idea.

With new information, however, the listener must construct a new memory structure to handle the idea, and that takes more time. The newer or more unusual the idea, the longer it takes. If the new idea can be related to an already existing framework, things go more quickly. Using analogies helps. The analogy provides a familiar framework against which a new idea is compared, sort of like a template for understanding. The learner uses the familiar framework to process the new idea and saves a step.

A key variable here is the audience itself. The "new" in this context means new to *this* audience. The most celebrated neurophysiologist might have difficulty keeping up with a rapid discussion of the dynamics of skateboards which any 12-year-old enthusiast would understand easily. The moral: if your lecture is going to cover very new ideas (or at least new to this audience), you cannot include as many ideas per unit time as you could if the ideas were somewhat familiar to the students already.

How much specialized or unfamiliar vocabulary do you use?

A corollary to the newness of the material is the familiarity of the vocabulary used to describe it. When students complain about the use of jargon, they usually refer to technical vocabulary. Although we bristle at the complaints and huff that they need to learn these terms eventually, we should stop for a minute and consider why the use of unfamiliar terms causes problems in pacing.

Learning technical vocabulary is like learning a foreign language. When you first learn a language, you hear a single sentence, translate it into English and then process it — a fairly slow and tedious procedure. And if a native speaker uses a word you don't understand, processing comes to a screeching halt while you 1) try to decide if you really don't know the word or just misunderstood the speaker, and 2) try to figure out what the word might have been given the context. Meanwhile the message continues on uninterrupted, and so you're likely to miss the remainder as well.

So it is when students listen to lectures using technical vocabulary. Until they become "fluent" in the language of the discipline, they spend a lot of time trying to "translate" what they hear into

English. And the more technical terms used, the more frequent the interruptions and the more complaints about the pace of the lecture.

What can you do about this? You can't stop using the terms, and eventually the students will become more fluent in the language. But in the meantime:

- be more patient with these "non-native speakers,"

- write new terms on the board, and

- pause after technical terms to allow for processing and minimize the disruption in the information flow.

Repeat, rephrase, and slow down whenever you use a lot of technical terms. Just try to think of your students as learning a foreign language, then react accordingly.

How complex is your material?

The complexity of the material — its underlying logical structure — greatly influences perceived pace. Ideas which have a simple, two-state, either-or structure can be presented in much less time than those which have a number of conditions and/or relationships which affect them. Complexity also relates to a concrete-abstract dimension. Ideas tied to concrete examples or easily visualized tend to be processed more rapidly by most listeners than more abstract ideas.

How complex is your sentence structure?

In addition to *material* complexity you need to consider complexity of the *sentence structure*. For example, sentence structures which contain a lot of dependent clauses and parenthetical expressions are much harder to follow when presented orally. We have a tendency to get lost somewhere along the line if the speaker constantly interrupts himself to go on a tangent. Lecturers come without instant replay buttons: we have to get it the first time around.

In written prose, complex structure is no problem because the reader controls the pace of presentation and can back up and reread a sentence when it gets too long. If a speaker's sentences get too long and complex, he asks the listener to retain too much in memory before he gets to the point. As a result the listener feels rushed or gets confused and ends up complaining about the pace.

This problem occurs more often when a speaker chooses to read a presentation, rather than giving it from notes. You must be an accomplished speaker or have a very good ear for verbal sentence structure to be successful at reading from a prepared script.

How well-organized are you?

Pace is seldom a problem when the lecturer has a solid and evident organization. From a learning standpoint, most listeners do not take in the entire content; rather they extract an outline of the main ideas. What gets filed away stands out from the background. The more readily the listener can discern the main ideas, the clearer the lecture appears. The clearer the lecture, the more appropriate the perceived pace.

Thus, anything the lecturer does to highlight the organizational structure of the lecture, the happier the listeners — and the better they learn. Use simple procedures to help the listeners follow the lecture:

- Put an outline up on the board, either at the beginning or as you proceed through the lecture.

- Make clear verbal transition statements, such as "the next main section is ...."

- Use visual aids to introduce each new topic.

Nothing fancy, nothing complicated. It's just like drawing a map: mark the essentials — the simplest maps are the easiest to follow.

How can you know if your pace is appropriate?

A few suggestions on developing a "feel" for pace:

- Encourage feedback from the students — and pay attention. The feedback doesn't need to be verbalized: you can learn a lot from faces, body positions and movements, and note-taking behavior.

- Visit another instructor's class, preferably in a very different discipline, and try to take notes as if you were a student. You can learn some surprising lessons this way.

- Audiotape one of your lectures and try to take notes from it at a later date. If you have problems, imagine what it might have been like for someone hearing it for the first time.

- Look at the notes students take during your lectures. What do they seem to be recording? Does that match what you would have recorded?

The question of pacing will be with us as long as we lecture. Perhaps we can best resolve the pacing issues if we view our lectures from the standpoint of our listeners rather than the standpoint of the speaker — and pace it accordingly.

An Instructor Survival Kit: For Use With Large Classes

Maryellen Gleason

Involve Students

Student involvement is decidedly harder to achieve with 200 students instead of 20, but it can be done.

The adept use of questions to stimulate interaction can be useful in large courses. Some instructors fear opening up discussion in a big class. What if everyone decides to make a lengthy comment? Clearly, that kind of seminar dialogue is not an option with 200 students; what is possible, though, is interaction with the class. For example, use a series of closed questions or queries to which a one- or two-word right answer exists. Direct questions to a general section of the class, not necessarily pinpointing individuals. Take even mumbled responses, repeating them so the rest of the class can hear. It's a good technique for warming a class up and reviewing earlier content.

Solicit questions for short periods. In mid-lecture announce, "Let's take five for questions." Respond concisely. If a student's question relates to content covered in an earlier lecture, politely point that out and suggest that the student check notes with someone else. If the question is a good one, say so. When responding, direct answers to the whole class. Remember, too, that no law dictates that only professors answer questions. Students will object, but with encouragement and praise you can get them responding to each other's questions.

Big classes require extra effort to counter students' passivity, to poke and prod students into states of mental involvement. An example: end a lecture by proposing, "Take two minutes and generate a test question on today's content that you think you might see on an exam." You might just get a good question; use it, and students will take those two minutes of class seriously.

Don't overlook the value of rhetorical questions. Many teachers use them, but the effectiveness is diminished by the way they are delivered. They need to sound like genuine, bona fide inquiries. Give students a few seconds to think about them. Point out that it is a question, not just a comment made in passing.

Interaction with students in large courses takes a certain amount of creativity and ingenuity, but the benefits in terms of student attentiveness and involvement can be high.

Resources

A four-page Idea Paper from Kansas State, "Questioning in the College Classroom," is a superior resource; Hyman has good suggestions for instructor-generated questions and for fielding and answering student questions. Monk recounts his experiences teaching a 350-student math course; it is especially strong on techniques for introducing student involvement.

Hyman, R.T. "Questioning in the College Classroom." Idea Paper No. 7. Center for Faculty Evaluation and Development. Kansas State University, August 1982, 1-4.

Monk, G.S. "Student Engagement and Teacher Power in Large Classes." In Bouton, C., & Garth, R.Y., eds., *Learning in Groups*, 7-12. New Directions for Teaching and Learning, No. 14. San Francisco: Jossey-Bass, 1983.

Use Small Groups

Small group activities don't automatically work well in any class, and especially in large ones. But the reasons are not intrinsic. Group tasks must be specific and concrete. "Groups should generate four possible explanations for the results we've just observed." Or, "In five minutes, I want each group to have a list of three items." Or, "Here's the statement .... I want to know if the group agrees or disagrees, and why." When tasks are not specific or clear, group members waste time trying to decide what to do, content-related discussion suffers, and students get frustrated. So, rule one is, make the group project specific.

Then, do something with group products. No one likes to contribute to an activity that nobody needs or wants. If students have worked on solving a problem, ask for their answer. If different answers are offered, all the better. Have group members defend and explain answers; take a vote. If groups have taken positions, have group representatives join panels to debate the issue. Collect lists, put them on transparencies, write them on the board, or whatever — but make use of what you have asked group members to do.

A word of advice on time and group size. In large classes, group projects work best if they are short — something quick and easy that adds presentational variety. Time allotted must be proportional to task, but five minutes can be enough to work on a problem. Discussions can be productive in less than 10 minutes. Tight time limits force groups to focus on tasks quickly. Shorter times work well if group size is kept small, to three to five people — or, on occasion people can work in pairs (although, in the latter case, it is harder to use all the group products). Group size is also proportional to participation; it is tougher to be a silent member when there are only two other persons in the group.

Sometimes instructors make too big a deal about group logistics — having groups move to this corner or that while distributing handouts and giving instructions about chair placement. Explain the task first — put it on a transparency, write it on a board, leave it visible throughout the activity. Then simply ask three people sitting near each other to join together. Get any "leftovers" together quickly. The goal is to move past the logistics swiftly.

More could be said about techniques, but the important point about using groups in large classes is to *try it*. They break students out of the passive-receiving mode; they encourage involvement and contribution. Groups attack the impersonality of large courses, and foster acquaintanceship and interaction. And, they force students to grapple, however briefly, with course content — to see, feel, and interact with it at close range.

Resources

Weaver sets out five objectives for small-group discussion, and proposes specific ways to accomplish them. Pulturak describes something he calls "The Colloqution Module," a method for using small groups in large courses. It incorporates reading and other activities into group experiences. Bergquist and Phillips present a four-page table proposing "Classroom Structures Which Encourage Student Participation." In it they list 10 different group structures, define each, indicate appropriate use, propose a preparation procedure, and describe its limitations.

Bergquist, W.H., & Phillips, S.R. *A Handbook for Faculty Development*. Washington, DC: The Council for the Advancement of Small Colleges, 1975. Pp. 118-121.

Pulturak, R.W. "The Colloqution Module." *Journal of College Science Teaching* 4 (March/April 1985): 421-423.

Weaver, R.L. "The Small Group in Large Classes." *Educational Forum*, 48 (Fall 1983): 65-73.

Develop a Style

Presentational matters include minor aspects of oral delivery that should not matter, but do. The fact that shoulders are hunched, eyebrows twitched, and words repeated should not count for much as against subject matter competence, but sometimes such idiosyncrasies of expression do impair effective communication — especially in large courses, where the numbers somehow exaggerate the errors.

The good news is that most distracting mannerisms are easy to remove once one becomes aware of them. The key is to step out of the action and see yourself as others do. Watch yourself teaching. Where are your arms? Where are you in relation to the podium? Always behind it? Listen to your words. How many times are they repeated? Where are your eyes? Are they in contact with individuals in front of you?

Presentation in large courses need not be substantially different from small classes. It should be an honest, authentic representation of the instructor you have discovered yourself to be. If you don't tell jokes in small classes, don't try to in large ones. If you rely on personal examples in seminars, use them in the big class.

Of course, not all presentational aspects will be the same in large classes. A microphone may be needed, overhead transparencies must be larger, and so on. In general, gestures and movements can be exaggerated in the larger class, and delivery more energetic; in big classrooms, there is lots of room to absorb the action.

There is no single, effective teaching style to covet or aspire to when teaching large courses. Effective instructors of big classes come in as many sizes and shapes as instructors generally. The key is to be yourself, to search for communication techniques that are comfortable and work for you, that maintain student interest, and that make it possible for students to come to grips with content.

Resources

Here are four good references on lecturing, plus one that recommends that you consider alternatives. There are two chapters in books: The first is Chapter 5 in Eble's *The Craft of Teaching*, which begins, "The best advice to the teacher who would lecture well is still, 'don't lecture.'" And the second is "Analyzing and Improving Classroom Performance," Chapter 4 in Lowman's book. Two articles are recommended: The first is a straightforward description of techniques by Weaver (who teaches large classes). The second, by Hanning, is a bit more theoretical, but it gets at the notion of "style." The "Alternatives to Traditional Lecturing" are offered by Brooks, who claims to have tried them with success in his large chemistry courses. Finally, if you feel particularly desperate about delivery, check out the book by Penner.

Brooks, D.W. "Alternatives to Traditional Lecturing." *Journal of Clinical Education*, 21 (October 1984): 858-859.

Eble, K.A. *The Craft of Teaching*. San Francisco: Jossey-Bass, 1976. Pp. 42-53.

Hanning, R W. "The Classroom as Theatre of Self: Some Observations for Beginning Teachers." *Association of Departments of English Bulletin*, 77 (Spring 1984): 33-37.

Lowman, J.L. *Mastering the Techniques of Teaching*. San Francisco: Jossey-Bass, 1984. Pp.72-95.

Penner, J.G. *Why Many College Teachers Cannot Lecture: How to Avoid Communication Breakdown in the Classroom*. Springfield, IL: Charles C. Thomas, 1984.

Weaver, R.L. "Effective Lecture Techniques: Alternatives to Boredom." *New Directions in Teaching*, 7 (Winter 1982): 31-39.

Personalize Evaluation

Given 200 students, an instructor can hardly construct an exam to meet every student's needs or provide specific feedback to every individual. Evaluation necessarily must be efficient and logistically feasible. Most often this means machine-scorable, objective exams with computer-printed scores posted for student perusal. The process is objective and efficient, but also cold and impersonal, and doesn't provide much feedback.

Again, small efforts can go a long way toward communicating an instructor's concern and commitment. Select a group of exams from every set to grade yourself. This allows a closer look at the kind of errors students are making and can deepen exam debriefs offered in class. More importantly, groups of students at a time get direct feedback.

If other graders have marked the exam, write a note of commendation on all "A" exams or on every exam score that has improved by a letter grade. This approach has many variations: personally return all "A" papers so you can commend students face-to-face.

If graders are used to alleviate the workload, it is imperative that consistent grading standards be applied as uniformly as possible. These standards ought to be shared with students. Some instructors employ a grade grievance policy that allows students to develop a case for an answer that may not have received the credit they deem appropriate. If instructors adjudicate this process, student objections can be put to rest, and it provides yet another way to communicate concern about student learning.

Pre-exam review sessions offer other opportunities. Announce that 30 minutes next Tuesday will be spent answering questions about material to be covered on the exam. Invite students to submit questions they would like answered during that time. If the questions are solicited beforehand, concise, clear answers can be prepared. Alter the tactic: ask students to submit the questions they would most like to see on an exam, use the review period to answer those questions, and demonstrate in the process how partial credit is assigned or what constitutes an "A," "B," or "C" answer.

Students are not insensitive to the constraints large courses place on instructors. They will notice and respond favorably to small efforts that guarantee the integrity of the learning environment and recognize their existence as individuals.

Resources

Effective testing techniques are important in any course, but especially in large courses where the opportunity to weigh exam responses by individual students is not an option. Lowman's chapter, "Evaluating Student Performance: Testing and Grading," is an excellent general reference that offers sound advice about virtually every aspect of evaluation. Because objective exams are a frequent necessity in large classes, an excellent article by Scott is referenced; it lays out a five-step process for the preparation of multiple-choice exams.

Lowman, J.L. *Mastering the Techniques of Teaching*. San Francisco: Jossey-Bass, 1984. Pp. 189-204.

Scott, A M. "Life is a Multiple-Choice Question." *American Historical Association Perspectives*, December 1983: 16-20.

Get Input

It is difficult to stay in touch in a big class, to find out what's on students' minds, to know when they are confused, outraged, or content. And yet that sort of feedback is crucial.

How can it be obtained? Foremost and fundamentally, from students. There are lots of options. A good starter may be some sort of student evaluation activity. Ignore the literature's debates about students as judges of instruction; students' ability to render descriptions of the effects of instruction is not disputed. And that's the information instructors need — especially if midcourse corrections are to be implemented. The point of an early student survey is to help you determine what you ought to do during a course — especially if things are not going well.

Instructors need diagnostic, descriptive details from students, and they probably need it more than once. Do the lectures facilitate notetaking? Is the pace manageable? Do the readings contribute to understanding of course content? Does the presentation style hold attention? Are the examples relevant? Are there enough of them? Is the value of the course clear?

Data like these can be acquired on an instrument compiled by the instructor — an instrument that asks what the instructor is most interested to know. As an alternative, a number of tried and comparatively true student evaluation instruments do exist and can be found in most books on student evaluation. Remember, though, the trick is to look for instruments that describe, not judge, aspects of instruction.

Student input gathered from a set of closed questions (like those on evaluation forms) has the advantage of being easy to tabulate and the disadvantage of being not very descriptive. Open-ended questions are the alternative. They can produce a plethora of details — so many, indeed, that an instructor can be overwhelmed. But open-ended questionnaires can be managed, even in large classes. Not all students must complete the questions. Probably all students who want to provide feedback ought to have the opportunity, but a survey of part of the class can be an option. Similarly, not every student need answer the same questions. If you're doing surveys more than once, sample a different portion of the class each time.

Open-ended questions can be *too* open — meaning you get everything from soup to nuts, including less than substantive comments. If you ask, "What did you like best about the course?" a student can answer, "The professor's socks." Open-ended questions, then, need a focus. Asking a question like "When do you find yourself most/ least intellectually stimulated in this course?" will give you a list of specific class situations that you can then accentuate or discard.

One can over-intellectualize the analysis of open-ended questions, especially since this is not strictly research. Student responses are best looked at as an idea source and identifier of major trends, matters apparent even in a cursory read-through.

The quality of data obtained from students will to a large extent be determined by what you do about it. Collecting periodic reports from students is well and good, but they need to know what you intend to do about the results. Discuss the findings and your plans with the class. It's a way of keeping channels open, and of making students understand that this is more than a clever activity to occupy idle moments.

Students need to know of the data's constructive use for another reason: to counter the strongly judgmental mindset that so often accompanies student "evaluation" activities. The point of the periodic surveys described here has nothing to do with judging overall instructor quality; the point is to obtain information about the course so that better instructional decisions can be made. When students see that as a result, succeeding surveys will bring from students higher quality and more constructively focused feedback.

There are, of course, many more ways to keep tabs on student reactions in large courses. Under "Resources," there is an article by a professor who monitors large sections of a chemistry course using the management concept of quality circles. Weekly sessions with a group of students are held to discuss how the course is going. "Are there problems with the reading for the week?" "Students typically have trouble understanding X. Have most students in our class mastered it?" Membership in the group can be voluntary, appointed, or rotated. Agenda items can be at the instructor's discretion or open. It's a novel idea with great potential for spanning the gap between faculty and students in large classes.

Resources

For general background on using input from students to improve instruction, see Abraham and Ost. Collections of student evaluation instruments have been assembled in many of the recent books on evaluating instruction, including *Evaluating Teaching Effectiveness, Successful Faculty Evaluation Programs, Developing Programs for Faculty Evaluation*, and *Determining Faculty Effectiveness* (which contains an appendix listing "facts about available student rating instruments"). Advice on developing your own instrument is provided by Wotruba and Wright. If you'd like to read how two instructors (who team-teach a 400-student course) use evaluations to improve their instruction, see "Never Wear Your Pink Shirt in the Forum: Student Evaluations of Teaching the Large Course."

Abraham, M.R., & Ost, D.H. "Improving Teaching Through Formative Evaluation." *Journal of College Science Teaching*, 8 (March 1978): 227-229.

Braskamp, L.A.; Brandenburg, D.C.; & Ory, J.C. *Evaluating Teaching Effectiveness: A Practical Guide*. Beverly Hills, CA: Sage Publications, 1984.

Brass, D., & Gioia, D.A. "Never Wear Your Pink Shirt in the Forum: Student Evaluations of Teaching the Large Course." *Organizational Behavior Teaching Review*, 9:3 (1984-85).

Centra, J.A. *Determining Faculty Effectiveness*. San Francisco: Jossey-Bass, 1979.

Kogut, L.S. "Quality Circles: A Japanese Management Technique for the Classroom." *Improving College and University Teaching*, 32 (Summer 1984): 123-127.

Miller, R.I. *Developing Programs for Faculty Evaluation*. San Francisco: Jossey-Bass, 1975.

Seldin, P. *Successful Faculty Evaluation Programs*. Crugers, NY: Coventry Press, 1980.

Wotruba, T.R., & Wright, P.L. "How to Develop a Teacher-Rating Instrument." *Journal of Higher Education*, 48 (November/December 1977): 653-663.

Check With Colleagues

Faculty tend not to talk much with each other about teaching — which is unfortunate. But the instructor suddenly thrown into a large class would be wise to initiate some useful dialogue. Most colleagues who teach large courses already have a set of survival strategies. Most are willing to share; all will at least commiserate; some may be confident enough to have you come to class. Do that. A "cook's tour" of large courses can open your eyes to a variety of approaches and provide examples and ideas not available otherwise.

Colleagues can help in other ways. One might take a look at a set of student responses to open-ended questions and give an objective outsider's opinion as to what they say. Colleagues in the same discipline are excellent sources of advice on content priority and structure. Colleagues can visit your class. They'll see things there differently from the student perspective, and in many respects are freer than students to call it as they see it. Maybe classroom visitation is an option only after you have your sea legs; colleagues can help, though, but you'll have to ask for it.

Resources

Colleagues' qualifications as assessors of instruction are well delineated by Cohen and McKeachie. Three books on faculty evaluation are listed: each includes a chapter with specific recommendations for the use of peers when the objective is to gain information that can improve instruction. See Chapter 4, Section 2 in *Evaluating Teaching Effectiveness*; Chapter 4 in *Determining Faculty Effectiveness*; and Chapter 4 in *Successful Faculty Evaluation Programs*.

Braskamp, L.A.; Brandenburg, D.C.; & Ory, J.C. *Evaluating Teaching Effectiveness: A Practical Guide*. Beverly Hills, CA: Sage Publications, 1984.

Centra, J.A. *Determining Faculty Effectiveness*. San Francisco: Jossey-Bass, 1979.

Cohen, P.A., & McKeachie, W.J. "The Role of Colleagues in the Evaluation Process." *Improving College and University Teaching*, 28 (Fall 1980): 147-154.

Seldin, P. *Successful Faculty Evaluation Programs*. Crugers, NY: Coventry Press, 1980.

Conclusion

Large course situations render instructional techniques used in smaller classes less effective. However, large courses do not automatically spell instructional disaster. The strategies described here are built on traditional teaching techniques, adapted to respond to altered circumstances. No one claims that teaching a large course is easy, but it is one of those academic necessities with which instructors committed to larger goals must cope. This "survival kit" can make the situation less traumatic for a first-timer, and turn a problem into an opportunity for learning.

Humor in the Classroom: Considerations and Strategies

Debra Korobkin

Shared laughter is a powerful way to reinforce learning, and it helps to make tasks less laborious and threatening. When students and teachers are questioned about what elements make learning exciting and effective, a "sense of humor" appears high on the list with other democratic, humanistic characteristics (Bryant, Comisky, Crane, and Zillman, 1980). The sense of humor is an elusive, seemingly inborn affective trait; its association with learning appears more linked with anecdote, myth, and naive optimism than with experimental findings. Yet, research does exist in which humor has been empirically and descriptively explored in childhood education and psychology literature.

Humor as a diagnostic and facilitating strategy for college teaching and learning is only now being investigated. Students and teachers with a sense of humor are sought after for their ability to set people at ease, equalize situations and status relationships, find unexpected connections and insights, and increase group rapport. Humor can be used to compliment, guide (Goodrich, 1954), or provide negative feedback (Coser, 1960), while maintaining goodwill (Kiechel, 1986). This article will examine these instructional implications of humor for the college classroom.

Humor in the classroom is a twentieth century phenomenon. Previously, it was considered unscholarly to use humor as a teaching strategy or even to show a sense of humor as a personality trait. Traditional subject matter and lessons were supposed to keep students interested (Wandersee, 1982). To entertain was not to educate. Thus, humor was viewed as an unnecessary and undignified embellishment of the serious, classic educational experience. Humor philosopher John Morreall recalls:

> The traditional attitude of teachers toward laughter and humor ... has been that they are frivolous activities that pull us away from what is important .... Life is fundamentally serious business — certainly whatever is important in life is serious business. If laughter and humor had any place at all, then, it was not in the classroom but outside somewhere, perhaps as a device for refreshing us to return to our work with more eagerness (88-89).

Collectively, teachers perceived instructing with a sense of humor as unprofessional, uncontrolled, and undignified. They avoided using humor in speeches, social intercourse and presentations for fear of being thought of as trivial, foolish, or ignorant. Humor was linked to mere popularity and likability. Similarly, college instructors made a conscious decision to be humorless because "serious professionals" conduct serious business.

However, in this century, the traditional classroom has been the scene of some changes. Humor and other forms of entertainment have been used and advocated even for the college classroom (Bryant, Comisky, and Zillman 1979). Laughter receives high marks from teachers and students alike because it unleashes creative thinking and reduces social distance.

Yet, even playfulness and creative imagination can be "put to work" in the traditional educational setting. Avner Ziv, an educational humor researcher at Tel Aviv University, states that humor facilitates

> the expression of a particular mode of thinking not bound to "right" and conventional answers .... Traditional education has been criticized often by many modern educators for its almost exclusive encouragement of the use of convergent thinking .... Divergent thinking can certainly be helpful in the educational process in such instances as problem-solving and all types of activities including self-expression (1976, 320).

The college student, who is actively engaged in skill building and self-growth, should find the creative and divergent qualities of instructional humor compatible with learning. The presence of laughter tends to open learners to divergent thinking previously suppressed by the critical, traditional self. New, often unlikely and outrageous ideas surface in this kind of environment as the "fun mood' increases creativity (Ziv 1983, 73-74).

Important to this liberation is the accepting and encouraging class setting that uses laughter to foster less conventional thinking. An instructor who actively shares in the humor helps to cultivate freer interaction, idea generation and group cohesiveness, while reducing social anxiety, conformity, and dogmatism (Ziv, 1976). Once the authority figure has given approval and extended an invitation to laugh, the resulting contagious effect has a "positive reinforcing effect on each member of the group, augmenting the enjoyment of all" (Ziv 1983, 74).

Research

Despite these observational studies, the actual empirical research investigating the relationship between humor and adult learning is negligible. While much research has been conducted using children as subjects, the major adult population that has been scrutinized for learning differences with humor is the college age young adult. These adult learning subjects were usually students in undergraduate psychology, speech and journalism classes (Gruner, 1967; Mogavero, 1979; Kaplan and Pascoe, 1977; Townsend and Mahoney, 1981). A better understanding of humor's relationship to learning is needed for students over high school age.

Still, instructional changes are occurring and being encouraged in the college classroom. Some of the alleged benefits of humor to learners include *increased*:

- retention of material
- student-teacher rapport
- attentiveness and interest
- motivation towards and satisfaction with learning
- playfulness and positive attitude
- individual and group task productivity
- class discussion and animation
- creativity, idea generation, and divergent thinking

Other benefits to learners include *decreased*:

- academic stress
- anxiety toward subject matter
- dogmatism
- class monotony

Measuring humor is a difficult task that can be determined by observation of smiles and laughter, self-perception surveys, and standardized tests on other variables. No standardized humor test is yet accepted. Then again, the perception of humor is subjective. The paradox of humor research is that the experimenters often must decide on what is humorous and then subject a group of learners to an allegedly humorous experience (Smith, Ascough, Ettinger, and Nelson, 1971; Townsend and Mahoney, 1981).

Humor, Retention, Anxiety

The short-lived pleasure of the humor response may have far-reaching consequences, yet only one study (Kaplan and Pascoe 1977) included a post-experimental follow-up of the effects of classroom humor. Researchers found no difference between "straight" and humorously presented information retention immediately after a lecture. However, upon retesting six weeks later, a small, but statistically significant, positive effect on content retention was found for students present in the humorous lessons.

Retention has a positive and close relationship with instructional humor. Mnemonic devices for jogging the memory have often helped test takers. For an instructor, the planned use of humor can spark student recall long after the lesson is over. Comedy writer Gene Perret (1984) says:

> If you as a speaker don't help your audience to remember your lessons, then you're wasting everyone's time. Humor, even if used sparingly, can help accomplish that needed retention.... Comedy is largely graphic. A funny image appears in the mind of the listener [learner]. We may paint this picture with words, but the real joke is in

the image that each person sees.... Most memory systems convert abstract ideas to familiar images because they are impressed upon the mind more easily and are retained longer. Since images are more easily remembered than are abstract ideas, and since humor is largely visual, it stands to reason that using comedy in an illustration will help people remember the ideas you are conveying longer and better.... Imagery is expressive, graphic and unforgettable (12-13).

Learning can become more enjoyable and less stressful in a laughter-filled class. These attributes can be critically important for potential dropout, high-geared achiever, developmental student, and social non-participant. These students may have problems, such as fear of failure, dislike of "school," reduced self-concept, stress over grades, and incongruence between self and the instructor (Long 1983). The seriousness and intensity of the instructional lesson create tension and mental fatigue. Attentiveness fades and anxiety increases.

Humor is a great remedy for tension. Just a touch can often relax and engage an audience so that people will pay attention and be motivated to listen and absorb. Humor is so popular and, yet so powerful, that when people hear it, they want to listen (Perret 1984, preface).

Norman Dixon (1973) describes the anxiety-reducing role of humor as threefold:

- Humorists broadcast a message that they can joke and be unafraid.

- Humorists clearly demonstrate their humanness and fallibility.

- The humor helps to diminish the perceived threat or fear.

This willingness to be spontaneous and "imperfect" enough to be able to laugh at self will better enable students to cope with self fears, reduce stereotyped perceptions of "school," create a dynamic learning environment, and foster a sharing and concerned attitude among all learning participants (Gilliland, 1971).

Engaging in Spontaneous and Planned Humor

Humor in instruction is not synonymous with classroom entertainment. Rather, humor is a variable that can be accommodated, understood, and applied to the educational setting. Laughter in the classroom can serve to revitalize the attention span and increase motivation, which can lead to increased productivity. Most would agree that increased productivity and performance are desirable, even if the process for attaining success is "laughable" (Welker 1977).

A college teacher can use knowledge of humor in diagnostic ways and for non-entertaining situations. For example, the absence of in-group humor and laughter in small group interaction may be an indicator of poor bonding. Low group cohesiveness can result in poor attendance, reduced productivity (Hare 1962), and individual dissatisfaction (Shaw 1976). An alert instructor can observe class humor for determining or diagnosing the health of the groups (e.g., punishing, cynical, and status-based humor versus accommodating, shared, tension-easing humor).

An important use of a teacher's sense of humor was identified by Rose Laub Coser (1960). She described the role of the "disguised moralist," in which humor is used to point out a problem while, at the same time, provide reassurance. Seemingly invaluable for stressed learners, this "safety net" function

combines criticism with support, rejection with acceptance. If negative sanctions are provided in a humorous way, a bond is established between the culprit and possible culprits — a bond that exonerates both, while simultaneous assurance is given that negative sanctions do not take place without social support.... Humor negates its own content. By ridiculing the victim it also informs him that it is not serious, that they can all laugh about it together. Humor permits one simultaneously to attack and to lend support (91).

For the individual learner, the establishment of an environment that tolerates and encourages humor seems to assist in learning the material (Mogavero 1979); social and academic barriers are lifted. This freedom serves to cultivate personal exploration, discovery, play, and risk-taking because the support system created by the shared group sense of humor allows for human error. When the inevitable error comes, it is received less traumatically. Students' satisfaction with learning is promoted because "laughter following humor has a liberating effect on the flow of ideas" (Ziv 1976, 319) rather than a punitive or judgmental effect.

Concerns About Humor Use

The instructor who wisely engages a sense of humor is not usually endangering his or her personal or professional credibility. In fact, trustworthiness ratings remain unaffected by humor use, while character ratings climb (Gruner 1967). What many teachers worry about in using a humorous approach (loss of intensity, reduced respect for the teacher, and weakened task orientation) simply does not occur when humor is gradually introduced, planned, and mutually enjoyed.

Obviously, there are real limits and subjective criteria that determine what and who is funny. Just because a speaker uses jokes and gags doesn't mean that the audience laughs or learns. There are real and perceived boundaries as to the appropriateness and type of humor used, style and method of humorous presentation, unhealthy uses of humor, implementation of the humor strategy, and cultivation of a sense of humor in teachers.

Although Don Rickles is a very funny and highly successful comic, his machine gun style of insult comedy would not be particularly productive for a group of learners. In fact, the most successful uses of instructional humor are those in which the instructor and learners are able to laugh together in order to learn together. Ridicule, satire, cynicism, and other forms of sharp "put down" humor can be punishing and non-productive if they are used often or in the wrong way. These forms of humor often indicate malice, or feelings of superiority and derision rather than supportive, empathic communication. A teacher or student who consistently finds himself or herself in a punishing "put-down" mode can see the humor as a warning indicator of deeper personal issues. Here, humor may be the result of darker feelings that have bubbled to the surface (Morreall 1983).

There are other forms of humor that reflect bad taste and bad judgment on the part of the speaker. Sexual joking is usually dangerous territory for an educator (Bryant et al. 1979, 1980). Similarly, ethnic, racial, religious, and other such forms of humor must be carefully scrutinized before they are used in an educational context.

Distraction from the learning goal is a danger in unrestrained humor use. On the other hand, distraction may lead to other worthy learning paths.

An instructional sense of humor may indicate that the speaker has the ability to see, to recognize, and to accept things as they are (Perret 1984). The sense of humor is a life outlook, an attitude, a personal karma. Humor is not just telling jokes, seeking popularity, pulling gags or using MTV to teach. It is a kind of presentation, a diagnostic strategy or activity that the instructor can use in order to promote comprehension, creativity, motivation, and delight. Some of the ways in which humor can be designed into instruction can include:

Promotion of a humanistic, laughter-filled learning environment. The instructor sets the tone of the class, and the students follow. If the environment is stuffy and dogmatic, little laughter and divergent thinking will occur.

For example, at the initial class meeting, an instructor can often use "getting to know you" warm-up activities to make the learning environment a comfortable place for new students. The instructor sets a tone that can influence the rest of the learning experience and the participation or non-participation of the hesitant learner. Don't confuse rigorous with inflexible and fear-provoking learning environments. College and adult students have academic anxiety and fears of "school." Try to ease stress and open up communication to reduce status tensions.

Cultivation of group humor. Classes often develop their own humor and in-group identification. Nicknames, group history and gags help to promote cohesiveness and directly affect task productivity and learner satisfaction.

The instructor needs to listen to the kinds of humor present in the classroom. Positive humor is evident when groups are working easily; individuals bond in group work. Punishing humor can be a sign of problems. Overuse of cynical, satirical and clownish humor may be an indicator of poor self-image, insecurity, poor group dynamics, boredom and misunderstandings. The absence of humor in small group and general interaction may be a key indicator of anxiety, low communications, low cohesiveness, reduced productivity, alienation, dissatisfaction and/or stress. The instructor needs to keep an ear out for the class clown and the class goat to ensure that they receive the respect due any learner.

Promotion of self-discovery and risk-taking. Learning activities that engage the humorous outlook are no more or less rigorous than "straight" activities. Rather, humor-based activities may require different problem-solving methods and communications processes than traditional activities.

For the college instructor, the self-discovery process may mean the adoption of new instructional methods instead of traditional or "safe" ones. Variety is particularly helpful to the mature learner who may have immediate applications and needs, as well as several personal learning strategies or styles.

For the instructor, it is not necessary to go to comedy school. Being relaxed, smiling and alert to learner needs are good starts to a better sense of humor. The integration of humorous stories and the promotion of class humor can be cultivated over time. Also, jokes and stories should be tried out ahead of time on family and peers (like a comic works an act) to make sure that they are humorous, content based, and non-insulting.

Some teachers develop joke and picture files for class use. Obviously the comic style is not for everyone, but a picture, cartoon or humorous story can be useful in helping students to remember a concept or for reducing anxiety about difficult content.

Development of retention cues. Humor can enhance retention by developing and promoting the use of funny cues. Incongruity in the rational world creates illogical, disjointed, and unexpected images that become memorable because of their graphic oddity. For the college-age learner, the funny images work most effectively when they are related to the primary intentional message content (Kaplan and Pascoe 1977).

For example, humorous images can be made into mnemonic devices. Many hapless test-takers have relied on seemingly silly word and image systems to jog their memory.

Release of anxiety and stress. While it is clear that the development of a sharing environment can relieve student academic anxiety, it is also clear that humorous strategies can be effective in dealing with and teaching about subjects that are considered taboo or highly technical. Family life and sex education units have been innovatively taught with humor (Adams, 1974). The approach is effective because the serious subject is lightened and made more approachable. Private and personal issues are more readily discussed because social barriers are lowered and participants are equalized in a trusting environment. Technical subjects are more willingly tackled because fear of failure is reduced by shared laughter. Group bonding and laughter reduce individual fears about highly technical or fast-paced lessons. Drudge work can be turned into a communal game.

Personal Humor Growth and Integration With Instruction

How can a college adult instructor cultivate his or her own sense of humor? How can this sense of humor be successfully integrated with sound instructional design? Even if the proposition that instructional humor is a good thing is accepted, how is the college instructor to put this idea into action?

The personal sense of humor can be developed in conjunction with the instructor's personal speaking and teaching methods. Some growth can be promoted through skill mastery in delivery and speech presentation. Many teachers seem afraid to let a natural sense of humor come through to students because the front of the classroom is already so intimidating. Reducing anxiety about presentation skills is an excellent start to developing self-confidence, shared humor, timing, and attention devices.

Awareness of humor can be a gradual behavioral process in which an individual develops a personal outlook on life that sees, recognizes, and accepts rather than judges and commands. Someone who can laugh at the trials and trivialities of life can help others to reduce their stress, to build self-confidence, and to be willing to try new things. Instructors can build safety nets for learners; individual imperfection becomes a step towards mutual understanding.

Integration of humorous activities and comments into an instructional sequence can be a slow and cautious process that requires a lot of trial and revision, like a comedy routine. Instructors need to examine the subject matter, their own personal brand of humor, their presentation skills, and their audience's needs in order to develop planned humor use — and occasional spontaneity. Presentation skills may be reviewed and sharpened. Eventually, a tried and true "straight" lecture can evolve into a more divergent activity that promotes student thinking, discussion, and motivation. Thoughtfully designed humor can be used as a strategy in activity development.

The college instructor can use the instructional design process in order to promote effective and laughter-filled learning. Part of the planning process deals with the generation of objectives, assessment of the activity, and development of instruction materials. Other parts deal with developing approaches to teaching and learning for the benefit of the learners. Instructional humor seems most appropriate to the latter functions of instructional design. (While it would be possible to generate funny objectives, their usefulness would not be any greater than for "straight" objectives.) Funny test items have been the subject of several research studies (Smith et al. 1971, Townsend and Mahoney 1981); it does not appear that, for the college age or adult student, humorous test questions are well-received or responded to. The intended humor does not significantly reduce test anxiety and may actually confound the student.

The role of classroom humor in college instruction and learning has barely been explored. Yet, there are positive implications for using humor in the college, professional, and graduate classroom if that humor is thoughtfully used in planned and spontaneous ways by the instructor. Particular kinds of learning may be significantly enhanced with the inclusion of humor and/or the promotion of class laughter. Students state that they find their learning efforts to be less laborious, more creative, more satisfying, and more memorable in the humor-filled environment; instructors often discover fuller learning relationships with their students in which the transmission of data is integrated with the discovery process and empathetic interaction.

Far from acting to alienate, subvert, or deride the educational experience, instructional humor seems to enhance learning. Classroom laughter can serve to liberate thinking, reduce academic anxiety, promote retention, and increase the learners' satisfaction with the experience. While not all teachers can or should act like Johnny Carsons at the blackboard, the thoughtful, spontaneous, or planned use of instructional humor can bring the wonder of play, wit, and wisdom into college learning.

References

Adams, W.J. "The Use of Sexual Humor in Teaching Human Sexuality at the University Level." *The Family Coordinator*, 23 (1974): 365-368.

Baird, L.L. "Teaching Styles: An Exploratory Study of Dimensions and Effects." *Journal of Educational Psychology*, 64 (1973): 15-21.

Bradford, A.L. "The Place of Humor in Teaching." *Peabody Journal of Education*, 42 (1964): 67-70.

Bryant, J.; Comisky, P.W.; Crane, J.S.; & Zillman, D. Relationship Between College Teachers' Use of Humor in the Classroom and Students' Evaluations of Their Teachers." *Journal of Educational Psychology*, 72 (1980): 511-519.

Bryant, J.; Comisky, P.W.; & Zillman, D. "Teachers' Humor in the College Classroom." *Communication Education*, 28 (1979): 110-118.

Busl, L.D. "The Teacher as Manager of the Learning Environment." *Journal of Nursing Education*, 20 (1981): 42-47.

Coser, R.L. "Laughter Among Colleagues: A Study of the Social Functions of Humor Among the Staff of a Mental Hospital." *Psychiatry*, 23 (1960): 81-95.

Demetrulias, D.M., & Shaw, R.J. "Encouraging Divergent Thinking." *Nurse Educator*, 10 (1985): 12-17.

Dik, D.W., & Warnock, H.P. "Enhancing Volunteer Productivity — Humor in the Bored Room." *Lifelong Learning*, 6 (1982): 10-12,23.

Dixon, N.F. "Humor: A Cognitive Alternative to Stress?" In Sarason, I.G., & Spielberger, C.D., eds., *Stress and Anxiety*, vol. 7, 281-289. Washington, DC: Hemisphere Publishing Corporation, 1973.

Emerson, J.P. "Negotiating the Serious Import of Humor." *Sociometry*, 32 (1969): 169-181.

Furlong, B. "Setting the Stage for Learning." *American Journal of Nursing*, 82 (1982): 300-301.

Gilliland, H., & Mauritsen, H. "Humor in the Classroom." *Reading Teacher*, 24 (1971): 753-756, 761.

Goodrich, A.T.; Henry, J.; & Goodrich, D.W. "Laughter in Psychiatric Staff Conferences: A Sociopsychiatric Analysis." *American Journal of Orthopsychiatry*, 24 (1954): 175-184.

Grotjahn, M. *Beyond Laughter*. New York: McGraw-Hill, 1959.

Gruner, C.R. "Effect of Humor on Speaker Ethos and Audience Information Gain." *Journal of Communication*, 17 (1967): 228-233.

Gruner, C.R. "The Effect of Humor in Dull and Interesting Informative Speeches." *Central States Speech Journal*, 21 (1970): 160-166.

Hare, A.P. *Handbook of Small Group Research.* New York: The Free Press of Glencoe, 1962.

Helitzer, M. *Comedy: Techniques for Writers and Performers.* Athens, OH: Lawhead Press, 1984.

Jackson, F. "Are We Boring Our Students?" *Nursing Mirror*, 17:35 (1983).

Kaplan, R.M., & Pascoe, G.C. "Humorous Lectures and Humorous Examples: Some Effects upon Comprehension and Retention." *Journal of Educational Psychology*, 69 (1977) :61-65.

Kiechel, W. "Executives Ought to Be Funnier." In Frost, P.J.; Mitchell, V.F., & Nord, W.R., eds., *Organizational Reality: Reports from the Firing Line*, 363-366. Glenview, IL: Scott, Foresman and Company, 1986.

Long, H.B. *Adult Learning: Research and Practice.* New York: Cambridge, 1983.

McGhee, P.E., & Goldstein, J.H., eds. *Handbook of Humor Research.* New York: Springer-Verlag, 1983..

Mogavero, D.T. "It's Confirmed: J-Students Like Humor in the Classroom." *Journalism Educator*, 34 (1979): 43-44, 52.

Morreall, J. *Taking Laughter Seriously.* Albany: State University of New York, 1983.

Perret, G. *How to Hold Your Audience with Humor.* Cincinnati, OH: Writers Digest Books, 1984.

Robinson, V.M. *Humor and the Health Professions.* Thorofare, NJ: Charles B. Slack, 1977.

Shaw, M.E. *Group Dynamics: The Psychology of Small Group Behavior.* New York: McGraw-Hill, 1976.

Smith, R.E.; Ascough, J.C.; Ettinger, R.F.; & Nelson, D.A. "Humor, Anxiety and Task Performance." *Journal of Personality and Social Psychology*, 19 (1971): 243-246.

Townsend, M.A.R., & Mahoney, P. "Humor and Anxiety: Effects on Class Test Performance." *Psychology in the Schools*, 18 (1981): 228-234.

Valett, R.E. "Developing the Sense of Humor and Divergent Thinking." *Academic Therapy*, 17 (1981): 35-43.

Wandersee, J.H. "Humor as a Teaching Strategy." *The American Biology Teacher*, 44 (1982): 212-218.

Welker, W.A. "Humor in Education: A Foundation for Wholesome Living." *College Students Journal*, 11 (1977): 252-254.

Wlodkowski, R.J. *Enhancing Adult Motivation to Learn.* San Francisco: Jossey-Bass, 1985.

Ziv, A. "Facilitating Effects of Humor on Creativity." *Journal of Educational Psychology*, 68 (1976): 318-322.

Ziv, A. "The Influence of Humorous Atmosphere on Divergent Thinking." *Contemporary Educational Psychology*, 8 (1983): 68-75.

Ziv, A. *Personality and Sense of Humor.* New York: Springer Publishing Company, 1984.

Heuristics for Creating Examples

Stephen Yelon and Michael Massa

Everyone tells instructional designers that good examples are important. Theorists tell designers to use examples for effective teaching (Reigeluth, 1983). Even students tell designers to use examples to communicate clearly and to make instruction interesting. But, instructional designers know how difficult it is to produce memorable, attention-getting and communicative examples because of the balance of technical requirements and the creative skill needed. However, there are heuristics that can help designers construct examples that are technically correct and creative.

The heuristics guiding construction of illustrations are based on elements of good examples. Just as a fine painting is seen as beautiful because it has certain elements such as balance, rhythm, and harmony, so does a fine example communicate because of accuracy, clarity, and attractiveness.

- Consider the *accuracy* of an example. Without accuracy, an example is likely to be counterproductive; students are likely to be misled and confused.

- Attend to the *clarity* of the example. Without clarity, students may not perceive the necessary message embedded in the example.

- Be mindful of the *attractiveness* of the example. Without attractiveness, students may not attend to the example.

However, a single example is usually insufficient to clearly illustrate an important idea even if it is accurate, clear, and attractive. Therefore, instructional designers must plan sets of examples. Without a set of examples from varied domains and of varying difficulty, students may have a narrow, simplistic view of an idea and be unlikely to transfer their knowledge to situations different from those shown in training. Thus, in addition to meeting requirements for accuracy, clarity and attractiveness, designers should check the transferability of the entire set of examples.

Heuristics Based on Elements of Examples

Using the elements of accuracy, clarity, attractiveness, and transferability, instructional designers can think about the creation of examples in an organized fashion. Let's consider the make-up of each element and how each may be built into an example of the concept of role conflict (see Figure 1). Figure 1 is structured to show the context in which the presentation is made, what the instructor says to lead into the example, the example itself, and what the instructor says to follow up the example.

Accurate Examples

If an example is accurate, students are more likely to understand the point. To produce understanding, examples should be appropriate for the type of knowledge, should fit the idea to be taught, and should fit its purpose in the lesson. Let's consider each characteristic of accuracy in more detail.

An example should be appropriate for the type of knowledge it represents. This implies that each type of knowledge, fact, concept, principle, and skill, has different elements. Thus, to prepare to create accurate examples, a designer must state the idea to be taught in a form appropriate to its type. For example, for facts, a designer should state the proposition to be illustrated; for concepts, a designer should state the definition of the category; for principles, a designer should state the definition of the relationship among independent and dependent variables; and for skills, a designer should state the steps of the process or the characteristics of the resultant product. The example of role conflict shown in Figure 1 is based on the definition stated in the lead-in.

An example should fit the idea to be taught. The elements of the examples should be analogous to the elements in the definition, the proposition, or the description. For instance, the attributes of the example of a concept should fit each characteristic in the definition. Note that the role conflict example has all the characteristics stated in the definition (see Figure 1). Specifically, the case contains two simultaneous pressures which conflict.

An example should fit its purpose in a lesson. Examples may be used to motivate, to explain, to practice, and to test. A motivational example emphasizes the positive or negative consequences of knowing the idea. A "best example" is a typical class member of its class, an epitome of its type, used to start an explanation (Tennyson and Cocchiarella, 1986). The role conflict example in Figure 1 would be used as a best example because it is typical of role conflict situations. Expository examples are complete, elaborated, and labeled instances which provide the substance for an explanation. Interrogatory examples are unlabeled illustrations to be used as a problem to be solved. Thus, when creating an example, consider its purpose in the lesson to adjust the emphasis and wording.

Clear Examples

If an example is clear, students are more likely to comprehend and to recall the statements and images which make up the example. Clarity can be enhanced by making the example concrete and brief, by including vocabulary and ideas known to the students, and by making the characteristics of the example apparent. In addition, when presented, the example should be clearly related to the point, should be shown in the appropriate medium, and should be related in a way so that it is clear what characteristics are being illustrated. Let's check each characteristic of clarity.

An example should be concrete. The words, images, or actions portraying an example should vividly refer to some observable referent. Use words which refer to some sensory mode: vision, taste, smell, sound, or feeling.

Use incidents, stories, and cases. Because the role conflict example in Figure 1 includes a dialogue between two workers and a part of a letter, a student should get a specific, clear, and concrete impression of the message. If the instructor used a more abstract illustration such as, "For example, a supervisor may be pressed to increase production while avoiding morale problems," a student might get only a vague, sensory impression of the message.

An example should be brief. The length of an example should be relative to the importance of the idea being illustrated. Cut out anything from the illustration unrelated to the elements. Note that in the role conflict example, every part is needed to complete the idea; for brevity, it excludes extraneous dialogue, and it includes only part of the letter from labor relations.

An example should include vocabulary and ideas known by the students. Scan the illustration for any unknown prerequisites. The role conflict example (see Figure 1) is understandable only to students who realize that increasing production and avoiding grievances are to some extent incompatible. Thus, giving this example to a junior-high school audience would be inappropriate.

An example should be displayed so that its characteristics are apparent. The essential elements should be accentuated or highlighted so they stand out. The elements should be made to be the "figure" while the case itself is made to be the "ground." There are several strategies for accentuating attributes: presenting examples and non-examples which systematically vary on the defining attributes (Engelmann and Carnine, 1982; Merrill and Tennyson, 1977), presenting a best example with annotations (Tennyson and Cocchiarella, 1986), and highlighting with colors, or simply pointing out the defining characteristics. In the role conflict example in Figure 1, the instructor points out the defining characteristics of role conflict as the example is explained.

An example should be presented so it clearly shows how its attributes or its variables relate to their corresponding attributes or variables in the definition. The trainer can explicitly reveal (visually or orally) to students how the parts of the example fit the point. Note how the instructor in the follow-up to the role conflict example highlights the attributes by pointing out exactly why this is an example of role conflict (see Figure 1).

An example should be presented in an appropriate medium. The example should be presented in the same medium or be as close as possible to the medium that a student will confront in the real world. Check the medium noted in the instructional objective (the medium should represent the best simulation of real conditions), and use that for the examples in the explanation. In Figure 1 the dialogue between supervisor and foreman and the transparency or the letter correspond to the conditions encountered by the trainees on the job.

Present a clear example of what is illustrated. To accomplish this purpose, a trainer should make a precise transition from point to example and from example to point (Gage, 1971). Note how, in the example of role conflict, the instructor provides a transition to and from the example in the lead-in and the follow-up.

Interesting Examples

When examples are interesting, students are more likely to attend to them and are more likely to be motivated to remember them. To be interesting, examples should be related to the experiences,

An Example of the Concept of Role Conflict

Context

Situation:

In a supervisory management course, the instructor gives the following example of role conflict. The students are experienced supervisors from an industrial setting.

Lead-In

Instructor:

"The next idea is role conflict. Let me give you the definition.

Role conflict — the simultaneous occurrence of two (or more) sets of pressures such that compliance with one would make more difficult, or impossible, compliance with the other.

What is a typical example of role conflict? Have you ever encountered one like this?

When I was at XYZ Co., I knew a foreman named Bill who had an experience which was a typical example of role conflict. First he had a discussion with his supervisor which went like this:

Example

Supervisor:

'Bill, your assembly rate has been dropping for almost a month. Last week's assembly rate was 25% below standard.'

Foreman:

'We've been having problems. There have been two machines down for maintenance. I've also had two men on vacation. As soon as things settle down ....'

Supervisor:

'I don't care about that. I want to see that assembly rate back up there now. You'd better find a way. I want your daily production figures on my desk every morning for the next two weeks.'

Foreman:

'Uh ... OK.'

Instructor:

That's the first demand.

As the supervisor walked away, Bill opened a letter from labor relations. In part it said (instructor projects a transparency of the letter using an overhead projector): 'This is the third grievance from your area this year. As you know, that is already one over your limit. With six months remaining in this MBO period, I don't need to stress the importance of avoiding any further grievances. I have suggested to your supervisor that you develop a plan which details what actions you will take to improve labor relations in your department.'

Follow-Up

Instructor:

That's the second demand, in conflict with the first demand. So, why is this an example of role conflict? Note how in this case there are two demands being placed on the foreman: for increasing production and for avoiding grievances. Furthermore, the demands are occurring during the same period. Finally, increasing production and improving labor relations are two demands which are, at least partially, in conflict."

Figure 1

91

interests, or aspirations of the students, should have novel aspects, and should be credible and realistic. In addition, to produce attention, examples should be presented in a novel fashion. Let's explore each of these attributes that produce interest.

Examples should be related to the experiences, interests, or aspirations of the students. Find the experiences, interests, and aspirations of the students, and then choose the examples which relate to them. The role conflict example which discusses assembly rates in Figure 1 is appropriate for its audience of supervisors from an industrial setting. In contrast, this example would have been inappropriate if the instructor had been speaking to principals who supervise teachers.

Examples should have novel aspects, i.e., examples should have some characteristics which vary from the usual or the expected. For this purpose, an example could include a twist of humor. Therefore, jokes, cartoons, stories, and funny experiences are good material for interesting examples (Cooper, Orban, Henry, and Townsend, 1983). If something makes you laugh, ask: What is this an example of? Then convert the joke, cartoon, or funny experience to an example to fit the point. In addition, when appropriate, such as after an introductory typical example, a whole unusual illustration could be used.

Events which provoke curiosity could be attention-getting, novel examples. Thus, examples could be selected because they describe puzzling or strange events. Examples could also have questions or puzzles embedded in them. Ask of each example: "For what question is this an answer?" Then pose the question before presenting the example. "What is a typical example of role conflict? Have you ever encountered one like this?"

Examples should be credible and realistic. The example should relate to real events when possible. The person explaining the case or story should have some personal connection to the event. Note that the example in Figure 1 came from the instructor's personal experience. Therefore, ask yourself, What experience have I had which can act as an illustration of the point? Then build the example to fit the point.

Examples should be presented in a novel fashion, i.e., presentation should include variations from mere exposition. The delivery of an example should be accompanied by the appropriate gestures and motions for a most vivid explanation. Look for opportunities where a character changes in a story, where a place changes, where there are opposing viewpoints, or where items are being enumerated. The instructor delivering the example in Figure 1 could use different voices for the roles of supervisor and foreman and could move from place to place to indicate role changes.

In addition, the voice tone and mood of the presenter of an example must be consistent with the message. Ask "What is the mood of the story or case?" and consciously portray that mood when explaining the example. The mood portrayed by the instructor in Figure 1 should be one of concern or worry.

Transferable Examples

To increase the probability the students understand the full meaning of an idea, designers should attend to the way they construct sets of examples. The examples should also relate to the aspirations, interests, and experiences of the students. Let's study in further detail the characteristics of sets of examples which relate to transferability.

Examples should range from easy to difficult. Early examples should be obvious instances, and later examples should be more subtle and more complex. Examples should gradually become more like the examples encountered in real circumstances. The instructor teaching the concept of role conflict would gradually introduce more subtle examples, perhaps embedded in more complex situations, or perhaps lacking only one of the defining attributes such as simultaneity of the demands.

Examples should represent varied situations and circumstances to cover the range of experiences a trainee may encounter. Consider all the places and times a trainee may encounter the instances of the idea taught, and have an example representing each one. Thus, the instructor in Figure 1 would want to provide additional divergent examples of role conflict, examples of different levels of management, and examples of different types of pressures representing the possible situations that supervisors may observe.

To be likely to transfer as well as to be attractive, examples should also relate to the aspirations, interests, and experiences of the students. Show the students the circumstances in which they are likely to encounter examples of the idea. Notice that the instructor in Figure 1 was getting two effects — transfer and interest — for relating the example to the trainees' past and future experiences.

Conclusion

Creating good examples involves a considerable amount of thought and skill. First, a designer has to be logical and precise in specifying the idea. Then the designer has to be intuitive and creative to produce the basic notion for the example. In addition, the designer has to use analogous thinking to make the example fit the point accurately and clearly. Furthermore, the designer has to be productive to make a range or representative and progressively more difficult examples. Finally, the designer has to use presentation skills to communicate the example in a clear manner.

Creating good examples is a continuous task. To some designers, this may sound like a chore. But this process is actually a satisfying activity that keeps designers fresh and interested in the substance of their courses.

References

Cooper, C.R.; Orban, D.; Henry, R.; & Townsend, J. "Teaching and Storytelling: An Ethnographic Study of the Instructional Process in the Classroom." *Instructional Science*, 12 (1983): 171-190.

Engelmann, S., & Carnine, D. *Theory of Instruction: Principles and Applications*. New York: Irvington, 1982.

Gage, N.L. "Explorations of the Teacher's Effectiveness in Lecturing." In Westbury, I., & Bellack, A., eds., *Research into Classroom Processes*. New York: Teachers College Press, 1971.

Merrill, M.D., & Tennyson, R.D. *Teaching Concepts: An Instructional Design Guide*. Englewood Cliffs, NJ: Educational Technology Publications, 1977.

Reigeluth, C.M., ed. *Instructional-Design Theories and Models: An Overview of Their Current Status*. Hillsdale, NJ: Lawrence Erlbaum Associates, 1983.

Tennyson, R.D., & Cocchiarella, M.J. "An Empirically Based Instructional Design Theory for Teaching Concepts." *Review of Educational Research*, 56:1 (1986): 40-71.

Successful Participation Strategies

Maryellen Weimer

Try these tactics *when you're directing questions to your students:*

Start asking questions early in the course. All sorts of norms as to acceptable and unacceptable behavior in a given course get set during those first few class sessions. If students learn they can wait you out, by silence convince you to answer your own questions, they will try hard to make you do that during the rest of the semester. But if you refuse to cave in (or do so only on rare occasions with magnificent protestation), you convey the message that you take questioning seriously and are determined to get answers.

Wait for the answer. We suspect most faculty don't. There is evidence that elementary teachers wait on the average about one second. That same research documents that when wait time increased to between three and five seconds, length of responses increased, failures to respond decreased, and frequency of student questions increased, among other findings. Obviously, we must be cautious when generalizing these findings to university faculty, but for verification we encourage you to check yourself and others you might observe teaching. Granted, the silence seems long, awkward and uncomfortable — but endure it. Wait patiently, smile, relax, and look as though you believe with all your heart that someone will help you out.

Ask only one question at a time. Sometimes in an effort to generate a response, instructors attempt to clarify a question by rephrasing it. That's fine — so long as the question remains the same. Often it does not. We have a great example on videotape where in the space of 28 seconds an instructor asks four questions. Upon writing those questions down word for word, we discovered substantive differences. Students do not understand that an instructor will take answer, *any* answer. They feel confused because they can't figure out what the instructor wants.

Don't answer the question, or answer only in the most desperate of situations. Look at it from a student's perspective. If you can get the answer straight from the horse's mouth, then you can dutifully record it, confidently knowing that you have the right answer. Students will wait a long time in exchange for this kind of security.

Try these tactics *when you're dealing with student answers to your questions:*

Praise right answers. Don't make a big deal over the student: that will cause embarrassment in the presence of peers. But praise the answer. "That was a good connection you drew between the historical and political implications." So often, really commendable student efforts get little more than a token "yes."

Be careful responding to wrong answers. Don't be dishonest by pretending the answer is right when it's not. Some instructors do this by not dealing with the answer. They comment, "Interesting. Anyone else have an idea?" Upon hearing the desired answer, the instructor then responds. And so, "interesting" becomes a polite way of saying "wrong." We advocate more direct honesty, but at the same time admonish instructors to beware. Students feel vulnerable when they answer in the presence of the professor and their peers. Even slight nuances in tone of voice or facial expressions can be devastating put-downs. Most professors don't call answers or students stupid, but many communicate that that's precisely what they think about an answer and the individual who offered it. Be assured that if you put students down, you will watch participation levels plummet — guaranteed!

Encourage more than one answer. Do that by not commenting on every student comment. No law says that for every student comment, there must be a response of equal (if not longer) duration. Collect a number of student comments. Condense and combine them, relating portions to each other.

Encourage a variety of students to participate. Occasionally one student (sometimes more than one) loves to participate. Ask a question, any question, and you can bet on her hand being first in the air. You and the class grow weary. Confront the student — preferably in private — with a clear statement of your concern. Explain that you greatly appreciate her willingness to participate, but that other students feel intimidated by her eagerness. You want to encourage them to participate, and if she'll exercise restraint on occasion, you'll be able to stimulate full class participation.

Equally important in cultivating increased participation are strategies for *answering student questions*. Sometimes they ask questions that aren't easy to answer. Consider these examples:

The question you can't understand. Ask the student to repeat or rephrase the question. Don't be afraid to admit that you don't understand. Be sure you don't imply you think it's a silly or stupid question. If you continue not to comprehend, enlist the aid of the class, or apologize to the student and suggest you need to tackle the question after class.

The question that is irrelevant — not bad but just inappropriate at this time in the course. Recognize the intrinsic value of the question when responding to the student, but don't get the class off track by answering it now. If you can legitimately consider it later in the course, tell the student when to expect an answer. Be sure to jot down the question and do your best to provide the answer when you said you would. You get even more points on that day if you can look at the student and say, "Bill, remember that question you asked about heat transfer in cast iron? I can give you the answer now."

The question you don't know the answer to. It's tempting to fake it, satisfy the student with fine-sounding terms and vocal authority. Don't. Be *honest*. No law decrees teachers must know answers to every question. You look human when you admit that, even in your field of specialty, some things you have yet to learn. You set an example when you return to class with reference materials that contain the answer. Better yet, involve students in your search. Invite them to the library to track down the answer with you.

The question that is stupid. There are some, despite what you may have heard. Take, for example, the student who asks a question you spent 15 minutes answering in class yesterday — and the student was in class. Or, the student who asks you to solve problem X when homework assignments for the past three nights included problems (and solved examples) of this very type. Is it right to take valuable class time to answer for one person in class what 85% of everybody else present already knows? No. Tell them where to find the answer, but don't take the time.

Questions that challenge your authority. For example, "Why do you make the quizzes so hard in this course?" "Are you ever going to tell us what we need to know from the reading?" These questions invite you to lose your cool. Don't. Stay calm. Smile, give the student as honest and reasoned an answer to the question as you can. Frequently such questions reflect a much deeper protest about the way things happen in the academic world. Politely decline the opportunity to debate. Settle the matter privately. Playing out professor-student altercations in public involves risks — even if you win.

What Can Discussion Accomplish?

Maryellen Weimer

There are many advantages in getting students more actively involved in and out of class. Discussion works well to cultivate the kind of involvement that leads to learning, but perhaps it would be helpful to be a bit more specific about just exactly what discussion can accomplish.

The clearest description we've seen appears in the Fall 1987 issue of the *Intellectual Skills Development Association Bulletin* in an article by Lee Humphreys, director of the Learning Research Center at the U. of Tennessee-Knoxville. First, "discussions can be used ... to discover just how much and how thoroughly students have mastered a body of material, methods, or skills." This may be the modern-day equivalent of the Socratic method, where teacher leads pupil through a series of inquiries to greater understanding. In the process, the teacher discovers the details of what the student does and doesn't understand. This is the way to explore how well the readings have been understood and can be applied.

The value of this use of discussion is, first, as feedback to the teacher, identifying what needs correction or further focus. The second value benefits the students, as they learn to respond to questions in front of peers and discover for themselves how comfortably they can handle the content.

Discussion also brings "members of a class into a closer working relationship with each other and with an instructor." Humphreys further explains the value of this use for discussion: "With so much academic work centered on the individual working alone, efforts that facilitate skills in working with others are more than justified." Discussion teaches students to listen to and respect the opinions of their peers. So often when a student makes a comment or responds to a question, students around the room act as though they've been given an unofficial timeout. People visibly stretch, yawn, and do not take notes. If the instructor doesn't always answer, or if students find themselves in activities where they must engage in dialogue with each other, they come to know and reckon with each other as fellow learners.

Finally, discussions can be used to further understanding — both in the students and the instructor. "We can ask questions about which an instructor may have thought, but for which she has not a clear answer towards which all others must struggle." Humphreys recognizes that differences in knowledge and depth of experience exist between instructors and students and encourages instructors to be honest. If we pretend the differences do not exist, or ignore them, we risk creating an "artificial context" that students will quickly discover. Truly exploratory discussions may not be as possible in introductory courses, but they certainly should be the *modus operandi* in graduate seminars.

Teachers can, and do, regularly learn from their students. The student insight may be incomplete or out of focus, but that is where the experience and greater understanding of the instructor benefit all. When a class works together to develop that further sense of understanding, a great feeling of accomplishment emerges. Perhaps this is where the love of learning — so missing in today's students — can be cultivated.

Group-Inquiry Turns Passive Students Active

Robert G. Kraft

Several years ago I won an award for "excellence in teaching." I know this is not a modest way to begin. I mention it because it created a problem for me. Students often assumed I was some combination of Bob Hope, Leo Buscaglia, and Albert Einstein. Of course they were disappointed, and sometimes they told me so.

And they were right, as I'm rather short on wit and humor. I'm too earnest and have a tendency to preach. In fact, I don't think students like me especially, but they like what goes on in my classroom.

What goes on is group-inquiry. Simply, my class is divided into groups of five. These groups are asked to inquire into the central problems of the subjects under study. They read about and write about these problems, then read their discoveries to their own group. Then they report their consensus to me and the rest of the class. At that point we all get a chance to challenge and modify. Later, they write new papers and argue some more. The whole process is busy, noisy, and powerfully effective.

It took me 13 years of study and classroom experiments to develop this form of group-inquiry. It came out of a conviction that students did not grow and develop, did not genuinely learn, with traditional teacher-dominated practices. I now believe such practices are obsolete and must be abandoned in favor of something like group-inquiry.

I've tried to describe the process to the many teachers discouraged with business-as-usual classes. But they are usually suspicious and reluctant, just as industrial managers often are with "participatory management." The program is so different from what they're used to; they simply can't imagine it. "How do you motivate students to do all that?" they ask. Finally they dismiss it as my unique style, not something they could use. That always disappoints me, but I know the habits of decades are not easy to question, much less dislodge.

Recently, the clamor for improved teaching has become louder. Also, some new evidence — one might even call it proof — suggests that the usual classroom practices don't work and must be replaced by something more active and involving. All this renews my hope, because the specific complaints are so beautifully eliminated in group-inquiry.

Passivity and Emotional Flatness

Complaints are coming from all over. Of the blizzard of K-12 education reports in 1983 — most of them not just critical but alarmed — the most substantial was UCLA Dean John Goodlad's *A Place Called School*. His immense three-year study concludes that secondary classrooms in the core subjects utterly lack effective learning atmosphere. Goodlad says these classrooms are monuments to "passivity and emotional flatness." They are dominated by endless teacher-talk and textbook exercises mechanically performed. Little in these classrooms will engage an adolescent's mind. As a consequence, "boredom is a disease of epidemic proportions."

Critics of higher education are acutely aware of the same problem. The National Institute of Education convened a Study Group on the Conditions of Excellence in American Higher Education. That group chose to call their 1984 report, "Involvement in Learning."

The study group recommends that faculty "make greater use of active modes of teaching and require that students take greater responsibility for their learning." The group specifically asks for "small discussion groups, especially in large classes," and for "in-class presentations and debates." Students must "hone their skills in writing and speaking, to extend their abilities in critical thinking and analysis." The NIE group insists that such approaches are essential because "students are more apt to learn content if they are engaged with it."

The Association of American Colleges Committee on the Baccalaureate Degree makes essentially the same points. They insist that "teaching comes first." They call for more inquiry and critical analysis through a celebration of "literacy: writing, reading, speaking, listening." Specifically, they urge faculty "to allow for more reading ... and fewer lectures, those invitations to passivity and pencil-pushing that are generally, although certainly not always, educationally counterproductive."

Once Again, the Failure of the Lecture

Past critics have also focused their complaints on the lecture. Yet the lecture dominates higher education and is often defended, mostly because professors have never seen successful alternatives. So they are unmoved when human development experts complain. In *The Adult Learner: A Neglected Species*, Malcolm Knowles says, "The best education takes place in nursery school and kindergarten.... It tends to get progressively worse ... reaching its nadir in college." Generally, such complaints fix on the routine, "pencil-pushing" passivity the lecture encourages. As a result, students disengage from genuine involvement and come to believe that learning is the same as note-taking.

The results are predictable. As Professor Lewis Schipper puts it, students "substitute mechanical learning for real learning. We emphasize extraneous motivation (exams, grades, credits, degrees), and students substitute short term memory for comprehension."

What to Do About It

But what to do about it? Most teachers have never been convinced there are better ways. Their own teachers — inspiring people among them — were lecturers. Other classroom practices they've heard of, or tried, seem no better, maybe worse. "Class discussion" often adds up to random and meaningless conversations with just a few students, many of whom are more aggressive than bright. And Socratic questioning generally falls flat. Since teachers know the answers, students won't offer any, because they feel they are being set up to look foolish.

Newer alternatives have been available for a long time, but they have rarely been put together in a coherent program or systematically demonstrated.

Group-inquiry is one such alternative. Most students find it irresistible and often ask me why everyone doesn't do it. They say, "It makes so much sense." It can be adapted to teaching any discipline. Teachers who understand it and try it never return to traditional practices, because it's simply easier and so obviously more effective.

But group-inquiry takes experimenting and getting used to. It's fundamentally different from what teachers and students have known. It requires that students take over much of what teachers did in traditional classes. The central problem of teaching, then, is the conflict between the processes of genuine learning and the business of schooling. A good teacher understands this first, and then finds ways to minimize this conflict. Group-inquiry is one such way. Students tell me they often forget about their grades in working together to find answers. And because of their higher involvement, they usually do better on exams and get higher grades.

But for all this to happen, teachers must understand precisely what they're after. Like coaches, they must have clearly defined goals; they must know what they want students to do, learn, and become. Vague goals like "an enlightened awareness of the subject" will not do.

Developing Skills

Although educators debate about goals, there are goals most of us agree on. We agree, for example, that students must develop certain skills to ensure continued learning and job success. In fact, employers and educators generally agree on the skills needed. When surveyed by a joint committee set up by Congress, employers asked for 10 basic skills in graduates. Of the 10, six are especially pertinent to group-inquiry:

- A functional command of the English language in its written and spoken forms.

- The ability to reason, solve problems, and understand the consequences of alternative courses of action.

- The ability to read, comprehend, and interpret written materials.

- The ability to write in a clear, concise manner with correct grammar.

- The ability to communicate orally.

- A capacity to deal constructively and effectively with others.

In traditional classrooms, only teachers practice these skills. They write, speak, consult, organize, and solve problems every day. Teachers become highly skilled. But students rarely practice any skills at all, except for an occasional paper or essay exam, done in isolation.

Group-inquiry, on the other hand, reverses the usual functions of student and teacher. The students conduct the class. They read, inquire, write, work together, and present orally. They simply take over. And they do it in *every class meeting*, in a structured series of activities defined and organized by a teacher who acts as a kind of chief executive officer.

Students discover that:

- They enjoy hearing the solutions of fellow students to the same problems they've struggled with.

- They can, in fact, come up with solutions, but they have to read closely and formulate ideas carefully.

- They must have a clear idea with some support for it, or no one will take notice.

- They have to write well to be taken seriously.

- They have some smart people around them.

How It Works

Here, briefly, is how the enterprise of "Introduction to Fiction" — of which I am chief executive — works.

I randomly divide my class of forty into teams of five. After reading a work of fiction, let's say, *Huckleberry Finn*, each team is assigned a problem, such as, "How does Huck Finn change as he goes down the river?" As homework, each team member reads, rereads when necessary, and writes a preliminary response to the problem. On returning to class, students read their responses to their team. The team members alternate to present their consensus response to the other teams who are working on other, related problems. A team may also ask students with the best analyses to read them to the whole class. Then the teacher and the other teams are free to affirm, refine, contradict, or debate what's presented.

All teams present their solutions in turn. After the class completes the process, students are asked to write another, more complete and refined response about any of the problems raised. These more finished responses are also read aloud in the individual teams; some are selected for reading to the entire class. They are also turned in for grading.

At first, student reactions to all this are mixed. A few resist all the required writing and speaking; they drop out right away. Many take to the program quickly; it's what they've always wanted to do. And there are always some few who disdain the notion that they should listen to other students' responses. They decide they will just wait for "the word" from me.

The great majority, however, are willing, curious, and decide to wait and see. At first they find the process of inquiry puzzling. School for them has usually been a matter of right answers to a teacher's questions. They are perplexed that there are no objective answers and feel a bit helpless. They tell me they're "ignorant" and apologize profusely. Often, after a preliminary "I don't know," they write some interesting responses.

After a few weeks of group-inquiry, all the students make some discoveries. Eventually, all the students come to like the program. Some complain that it's not going on in all their classes. The results — short- and long-term — are most gratifying. No student has ever reported disappointment in the course. (Some have reported disappointment in *me*. But they readily separate me from the course.) No student has ever reported a preference for traditional approaches. On the contrary, enthusiasm for the program has been consistently high, even after the course has been over for some time. In recent months, I've encountered three students who were in past classes, one of them seven years ago. All three mentioned a work of fiction from the class, how they still think about it, use it, or how they are reminded of it in something they've felt or observed. And the ultimate reinforcement for me: one student told me he has changed his major to literature and he'd like to be a teacher.

Why Group-Inquiry?

Group-inquiry works so well because it's based on learning principles we all recognize. The principles remind us of how and why *we* learned. These are most important:

- Students must be genuinely interested in what they're learning, apart from exams, grades, degrees and the paraphernalia of school.

- Students are most interested when subjects are defined in terms of experience and concrete problems. That's why case studies are so useful. Abstract discussions do not sustain interest for long.

- Students must dig out and test their own answers. Answers from authorities are not internalized and are quickly forgotten. That's why lectures and textbooks have limited use.

- Students are most likely to think about their subjects when asked to write and speak. Thinking is composing; composing is thinking.

- Students learn most permanently and with most pleasure in concert with other students. We all learn alone, but learning with others powerfully enhances learning and is crucial for most students.

- Students learn most permanently in an atmosphere of high feeling: enthusiasm, joy, even anger. Teachers must acknowledge and encourage genuine feeling of all kinds in the classroom.

- Students will learn most permanently and are encouraged to learn more when their learning is rewarded. Threats and punishment have uncertain effects. Often, punishment kills the desire for further learning.

- Students are most committed to learning when they participate in planning and organizing their learning.

The Teacher's Role

My role in all this involves less work than in my earlier, traditional approaches. But group-inquiry is *much* less burdensome for me because the students carry most of the responsibility to make it all work. Planning is easier because there is a pattern of activities everyone knows and follows. And group-inquiry is certainly more stimulating.

But some teacher tasks continue. I give some introductory lectures to explain the hows and whys of the program. I present all necessary information — material I used to lecture about — in printed handouts and, in some classes, a coursepack. I also write analyses of some of the problems I assign and then read them to the class, so students can observe how I do them. Finally, I referee their discussions, usually to paraphrase their remarks in terms everyone will understand easily.

I give no quizzes and few exams. I respond to all papers and carefully review the finished ones. My primary job is to organize all this, define, and assign the problems, which must have these features:

- Pertain to the central issues of the course and the work under study.

- Be written simply and clearly.

- Be open-ended, that is, they must allow for a number of possible responses.

- Require close observation and analysis; they cannot be simply "fact" questions with clearly right or wrong answers.

- Have a certain natural appeal, a "real-life" interest which can comfortably engage students.

At first, preparing all this material was no easier than preparing lectures. But I find I only need to do it once. In the following semesters I only refine the problem questions, or add and subtract as necessary. The rest of the program requires little preparation unless I introduce new material. Mostly, I have to keep the program running smoothly.

I have some ways to grease the wheels. Group-inquiry seems to work best in an atmosphere of first-name informality, even festivity, so I introduce myself and ask for introductions all around. I encourage everyone to be open and personal. I also praise and reinforce whenever honestly possible — which is *often*.

I reshuffle the teams once or twice during my fifteen-week term and serve as trouble-shooter and resource person. As the term moves along I do less and less. When students get comfortable with the program, I like to add variety. I ask for panel presentations and other special performances. Any glitches in the program are discussed with the class. All "fixes" come out of class consensus.

The long-term consequences for me are that teaching has become unpredictable and, so often, surprising and exciting. I don't get bored; I never worry about burnout. And there have been more tangible rewards, such as the aforementioned annual award for "excellence in teaching," won largely because of student testimonials.

So, of course, I believe in group-inquiry for any teacher. As long as a teacher understands and commits to the learning principles operating here, and the specific skills students must practice, all kinds of variations are possible. Group-inquiry works especially well because it makes every student active and visible. The challenge in the problem-solving, added to the constant and competitive social interchange, generates an interest no teacher alone can duplicate. However inert some students are inclined to be, they find it hard to stay uninvolved.

Who Says It Works?

How do I know group-inquiry works better than traditional practices? I want to answer, "Ask my students." But since you can't do that, a quick review of a University of Chicago study may do as well.

Professor George Hillocks, Jr., working under a grant from the Spencer Foundation, conducted a "meta-analysis" called "What Works in Teaching Composition." He examined over 500 experimental studies conducted between 1963 and 1982. He tried to find out what kind of classroom practices produced the greatest gains in the quality of student writing. He did a careful statistical analysis, rigorously controlled for the countless variables involved.

Hillocks found that the usual "presentational" way of teaching, "emphasizing the role of teacher as presenter of knowledge, including lecture and teacher-led discussion" was *ineffective*, producing either slight gain or no gain at all. Some of the presenter's class activities, notably workbook exercises in grammar and mechanics, actually resulted in a net loss in the quality of student writing.

Hillocks found that all other ways of teaching were more successful. Even unstructured classes, in which students got together to read what they had written and congratulated each other, produced greater gains than the presentational.

One way of teaching was dramatically more successful than all others. It produced a difference in effect three to five times greater than all other ways. Hillocks calls it "environmental." In his description you will recognize group-inquiry:

> "Environmental" emphasizes specific objectives with materials and problems selected to engage students with one another. Teachers minimize lecture, but structure activities so that students work on particular tasks in small groups before proceeding to similar tasks independently. While teachers provide brief introductory lectures, principles are not simply announced and illustrated, but are approached through concrete problems, the working through of which not only illustrates the principles, but engages students in their use.

Hillocks concludes, "Clearly, the environmental mode is responsible for higher gains than the other modes."

I'm not aware of massive studies like this in the teaching of other disciplines. But this study is relevant to all teaching.

The Unmajor

I once met a clothing salesman who told me he had a degree in history. I brought up the Russian Revolution, but he seemed to have little interest, recall, or sense of that event. I got off the subject quickly when he said, "I guess I've forgotten all that."

He majored in history but never got involved in it. No one ever asked him to. He was only asked to take some courses, some notes, and some examinations. If you talk to enough people about what they studied in school, you will find that this history unmajor is the rule, not the exception.

If teachers and schools are to improve, educators and the public at large must surrender some comfortable assumptions. They must give up notions that students have learned because they: were told; took a course; attended class, read the text, and listened; scored well on exams; and/or have diplomas and degrees.

Students learn only because they want to, deeply care to, and invest themselves in it. We can no longer afford to *hope* they will care and invest. They won't. Not if we continue the same deadly routines in school.

SECTION 4

Evaluating the Results of Your Teaching

You evaluate the results of your teaching when you evaluate the accomplishments of your students. The grades and feedback you provide give students an indication of how well they have succeeded with your content — but their success (or failure) is also a reflection of your success (or failure). That does not mean you anguish endlessly, especially over a student who failed without expending effort. But when 50% of a class fails an exam you must realize that, despite your best attempts to communicate content and to provide opportunities to develop the necessary skills, half the class did not succeed. We think it's unrealistic and unfair to assume all the responsibility, for that belongs to them.

If you find yourself arguing with us at this point, before you decide we're wrong, you need to read the first article in this section, which tackles the many thorny issues related to grades and what they do and do not "measure." Pollio and Humphreys explain a bit more graphically, "Grading outstrips both intercollegiate athletics and intramural sports as the most frequently played game on the college campus. It takes place in all seasons, and everyone gets to play one position or another. As in other sports, the grading game yields a plethora of statistics, around which has developed a distinct and mystical numerology." (p. 109)

The article on "Grading Students" puts the process into perspective and at the same time makes it clear that "grades, grading and the use made of them strongly affect the academic climate within which teaching and learning take place." (p. 109) But that larger context needs at this point to give way to consideration of more specific evaluation activities — like exams. Almost all instructors use them, and almost all instructors and students do not find them particularly constructive experiences.

For students the overwhelming concern is the grade. "Whatcha get?" echoes around the classroom when papers are returned. For instructors the overwhelming concern is what the students learned, but all too often only the teacher asks that question. The bridge between those two perspectives can be built if instructors seek to weave exam experiences into the warp and woof of a course. They need to create accurate expectations about exams, at the beginning of the course and before each exam, and help guide the review and study process. They must construct good exams with carefully planned questions, problems and other items. And they must consider different strategies for going over the results with students. Do all that and McMullen-Pastrick and Gleason contend, "Careful and sensitive planning, preparation, and processing of exams can make them a vital part of teaching and learning." (p. 121)

To illustrate two aspects of the exam experience more fully, consider how exam review sessions can be conducted and how multiple-choice exams can be improved. Writing multiple-choice items is far more taxing than most teachers first realize. Clegg and Cashin offer particularly sound advice.

We are strong proponents of interactive activities for students and equally convinced that they deserve feedback on their mastery of content as demonstrated through these activities. But how in the world do you grade participation?

Not as most instructors do. Most college teachers today have discovered that students participate more in classes if they get credit for doing so, and consequently participation "counts" in many classes, commonly somewhere between 10% and 20% of the final grade. How that gets calculated remains a mystery. Certainly the students are not apprised of the criteria used and only rarely are they provided any direct feedback as to their participation performance. More often, instructors use participation credit as a "fudge factor" of sorts, boosting the B to a B+ if the instructor thinks the student participated enough. Lyons and Clarke offer much more constructive approaches to this dimension of evaluating students.

We started out by asserting that self-evaluation needs to be a part of an instructor's evaluation activities with students. You may recall we started Section 1 by raising the same issue. How do college teachers judge their effectiveness? By looking at how well their students performed in class, and yes, by listening to feedback others offer about the teaching.

The problem here is that first teaching experiences are seldom the best of all the teaching that will be done. Those of us who have been teaching for some years look back at our first attempts with a certain chagrin and embarrassment. (But then we didn't have a volume like this to help us avoid the customary first-time-through pitfalls.) What we are gently trying to tell you is that somebody (student or more experienced instructor) may criticize your teaching. If that happens, you need to know how to learn from that experience.

But more important than knowing how to respond to criticism is knowing how to make changes, how to improve. The good news is that teaching is like running, writing, swimming, painting and a host of other skills: with practice, patience and persistence your teaching will improve.

Grading Students

Howard R. Pollio and W. Lee Humphreys

Grading outstrips both intercollegiate athletics and intramural sports as the most frequently played game on the college campus. It takes place in all seasons, and everyone gets to play one position or another. As in other sports, the grading game yields a plethora of statistics, around which has developed a distinct and mystical numerology. A conservative estimate suggests that with roughly 12 million students enrolled in two- and four-year institutions of higher education in the United States, and with each student taking three or four courses per term, between 72 million and 96 million final course grades are assigned each year. There is no telling how many individual grades are given for specific assignments, tests, papers, lab reports, projects, public performances, class participation, and even attendance. Once given, these grades generally are blended into a single number called the grade point average (GPA), which is taken to the second decimal or beyond. We all are aware that very important decisions that profoundly shape the future lives of students may be made on the basis of the GPA.

Grades, grading, and the uses made of them strongly affect the academic climate within which teaching and learning take place. With the exception of very few institutions, grades and the grading game are basic facts of academic life for professors and students, and they influence in many and varied ways important interactions between teachers and learners. We want to argue that we should do everything possible to ensure that grades and grading enrich the academic setting, facilitate fruitful interactions between instructors and students, and serve to augment rather than impede the course of college learning. We can begin by reflecting on some things everyone "knows" about college grades, to see if new implications may be drawn from these familiar facts.

Common Knowledge About Grades

There is nothing esoteric about the following five facts; they are simply common knowledge that students, instructors, and administrators share about grades. Even though they are known, we may not understand all they imply.

Different instructors produce grades in different ways. As college professors, we have received and given grades. From both perspectives, we know that some instructors grade against an absolute standard and measure student products against this norm, others allocate grades on some sort of curve that ranks each student in relation to his or her peers, and still other instructors stress the amount of growth or development a student demonstrates (that is, they grade the degree to which potential has been developed or realized). Using any of these methods, it is always possible to nuance grading still further by taking account of such factors as class cuts, tardiness, absence due to illness, personal problems, and so on.

The meaning of any grade assigned to a student depends in part on the priorities or the individual instructor who gives it. Grades are determined by the values of individual instructors who teach individual disciplines, and these values give grades their specific operational form. How we grade reveals what we value. Most of us who give grades find that as the grade leaves our hands, and certainly as it leaves our classroom in the form of a final grade report, all indications of the unique procedures and values underlying it are stripped from the notation. A single letter on a transcript bears no trace of the way in which that grade was produced nor of the instructor's procedures, priorities, and values. An A from one professor is not the same as an A from a second professor.

The quality, nature, and number of classroom tests vary. Instructors may take account of many things when they assign grades, but tests usually have a central position. It is no secret that the quality, number, and nature of classroom tests vary from class to class, discipline to discipline, and college to college. Some instructors let it all ride on a final exam, some give a midterm and a final, and some use frequent quizzes. Some instructors prefer essays, while others prefer "objective" tests, generally of the multiple-choice variety. Some essay tests tap little more than simple recall, asking only that the student give information in sentences and paragraphs. Some essay questions seem well-designed and focused; others are so vague as to invite the strategic nonsense some students become adept at producing. Multiple-choice tests normally ask for recognition of items rather than recollection, and studies indicate that most of them tap little more than recognition (Milton, 1982). Indeed, it takes thought and practice to produce multiple-choice items that involve higher orders of critical and creative thinking. Most faculty have had little training in constructing such test items, and too few discuss classroom testing with colleagues, even though there is ample evidence, both long-standing (Class, 1935; Balch, 1964; Hakstian, 1971) and of more recent origin (Milton, 1982; Eison, Pollio, and Cunningham, in press), to indicate that what and how we test is a powerful force in shaping what and how students learn. Certainly what is tested and how it is tested is rarely apparent in a grade notation, especially outside the immediate classroom context. The testing procedure vanishes when the grade is buried in the transcript and in the GPA.

Cheating goes on in college classrooms. Attempts to prevent cheating are many, and some are so elaborate as to distort the context for teaching and learning. Yet cheating goes on anyway. A recent national survey of attitudes toward grades and grading (Milton, Pollio, and Eison, 1986) indicates that over one-half of students surveyed reported having cheated to improve a grade. When faculty, parents, and business groups were asked the same question, the values were 36%, 34%, and 42%, respectively. The present generation of students does not have a monopoly on cheating, even if their elders seem a bit less guilty. Students recognize in this perverse way that grades are powerful and valuable tokens.

The pedagogical practices of many faculty members reinforce the message that grades are important, and parents as well as others add their weight to this view. Questionnaire results reveal that grades are valued by students, their parents, and others as symbols of much more than test results or academic attainment. Pollio, Humphreys, and Milton (1987) found that these groups believe that grades reflect such personal traits as psychological adjustment, the ability to work in a system, intelligence, self-discipline, and personal motivation. If these connotations are not enough to indicate how significant grades are to all players in the grading game, it is also clear that important extracollegiate decisions are made on the basis of grades. A person's GPA can open or close doors of opportunity that may determine the course of his or her professional and personal life. Even such crucial issues as the cost of a student's auto insurance are influenced by the GPA. It's little wonder that students are tempted to cheat.

Grading stakes are high for faculty and students alike. Little can rival the grading game as a wedge in relationships between instructors and students. No other factor is as powerful either in leading students to subvert the academic process in leading faculty to behave in an autocratic or adversarial way. There may be areas where faculty and students perceive certain actions differently with regard to whether they constitute cheating (for example, collaboration; see Barnett and Dalton, 1981), but there are others where all agree on what constitutes cheating, and such activities are not uncommon in the classroom.

Some students are interested in making grades but not in learning. With stakes so high, for some students the grading game has taken on a life of its own, distinct and separate from learning. On the basis of the way in which students answered a questionnaire designed to determine orientation toward both learning and grades, researchers have come to classify students as learning-oriented, grade-oriented, or some combination of the two (Milton, 1982; Milton, Pollio, and Eison, 1986; Eison, Pollio, and Milton, 1986; Eison, Pollio, and Cunningham, in press). In practice, four different groups of students are defined by the combination of being high or low on both grade and learning orientations. Perhaps the single most revealing way to spot a grade-oriented student in the classroom is to notice who asks the dreaded question "Will that be on the exam?" A negative answer invariably leads to an immediate and irrevocable loss of the student's interest, no matter how brilliant the instructor's presentation.

Characterizing someone as a high or low grade- or learning-oriented student has been shown to relate to the ways in which that student performs in class and to what he or she values about this experience. For example, Eison, Pollio, and Cunningham (in press) found that students with a high grade orientation prefer multiple-choice exams more than students with a learning orientation do; they state that they usually find such tests easier to take or that they have done better on them in the past.

Not one grade-oriented student selecting a multiple-choice test felt it fostered better or more significant learning. In contrast, students with a stronger orientation toward learning than toward grades indicated greater preference for essay tests, and while they gave similar reasons for their choice of test format, some suggested they felt essay tests better reflected their abilities and that preparing for such tests facilitated learning.

In another study designed to determine what students did and thought about during lectures (Pollio, 1984), grade-oriented students were found to be off target more than learning-oriented students were. Even when grade-oriented students were perceived by a trained observer to be on target in terms of what they were doing, they were off target in their self-reports of what they were paying attention to a significant percent of the time. The grading game is so intense that for some students attaining a good grade stands in direct competition with the cardinal purpose of higher education: to learn all you can, whether the information will be tested or not.

College professors got better grades than anyone else. While for a number of students grades themselves are significant enough to detract from learning, most instructors know that students do not really value grades as highly as they themselves do. This may be largely because college professors tend on the whole to have been winners in the grading game. Results of a national survey (Milton, Pollio, and Eison, 1986) revealed that 61% of 854 current faculty members reported having received "mostly A's" in college. Comparable values were 23% for 4,365 current students, 25% for 362 business recruiters, and 32% for 584 parents. We will describe some of the specific ways in which faculty differ from students and others in their perceptions of grades; that such perceptions vary comes as no surprise. We have all known students who are driven by grades and who nevertheless perceive grades as tokens of little worth in themselves or in relation to learning, but of immense value in the larger struggle for position and privilege — a struggle in which colleges and universities serve more and more as institutions for sorting, ranking, and selecting people.

These brief reflections on things everybody knows about grades suggest above all else that they are context-determined phenomena. The meaning of a grade depends on the factors that determine the specific climate of the class in which it is assigned. Primary among these factors are the priorities and procedures that instructors use in assigning grades, as well as the nature and quality of tests and other assignments on which the grade is based. There also seem to be marked differences in the meaning grades have for professors and students, with professors overvaluing their own symbols. Grades may appear to be context-determined symbols for communication between teachers and students, but on transcripts and in the GPA they have taken on a weight and a life of their own, quite distinct from and even in competition with their uses in teaching and learning. This state of affairs has led same students and instructors into practices that are inimical to the academic climate of cooperation and mutual trust that facilitates genuine learning. Cheating becomes commonplace, and learning takes second place to grading.

Uncommon Knowledge About Grades

A more effective use of grades in teaching and learning can be approached by considering additional information about grades, information that may not be very well known.

Grades did not always have the five major categories A through F. In the history of higher education, letter grades are relative latecomers, especially in the form we know them today. In 1783 the first grades in this country were given at Yale. Four categories — Optime, Second Optime, Inferiors, and Pejores — were used to describe the totality of a student's year. One suspects that deportment and decorum were as formative as academic attainment in shaping the grade. It was not until a century later that the first letter grade — a B — was given at Yale. Over the next century, there were marked swings in the number of units that defined the various grading scales employed (see Milton, Pollio, and Eison, 1986). These ranged, for example, from two units (Pass/Fail or Pass/No Credit) in the '60s and early '70s of this century to a system with five to thirteen units (A through F, often with pluses and minuses) to one with 100 to 400 units (percentages, or the 0.00-4.00 scale used by some law schools).

Grades were not always as pervasive a part of academic life as they are now and in the form we give them today. Even more interesting, regular swings in the number and nature of grading systems seem to correspond to larger swings in societal concern for standards, accountability, and the ranking of people on the one hand, and individual growth and group consensus and support on the other. Grading systems reflect a contrast — between competitive ranking and cooperative support — that pervades our society more generally. Through the grading of students and the use made or allowed to be made of grades, higher education has responded to and been shaped by larger societal and historical trends. Grades, which serve as a mode of communication in higher education, have become reified (above all in the GPA) and are used to sort and rank people for jobs, professions, and often the advanced training needed to enter them. Grades often skew the academic climate, and the manner in which the grading game has come to have a life of its own can be traced to these latter uses of grades.

Do we really need so many units in our grading systems if we use grades to communicate with students about their mastery of material and skills in specific courses? Some instructors may be comfortable employing more categories (A through F, complete with pluses and minuses); others may find Honors, Certified, and Not Certified enough. Instructors should never be required to use scales more finely calibrated than their powers or desires to discriminate among students. Our tests should be designed to tap significant information and permit students to demonstrate knowledge of important material and skills. We will not need to tap trivia, or to test obscurities buried in footnotes, if we avoid the trap of ranking all our students and making the minute discriminations required to assign positions on some multiunit scale. We do not argue here for a standard number of units; this decision should be made by the individual instructor. What we do suggest is that the symbols used to communicate between teacher and student not exceed the instructor's power and need to discriminate. Our primary purpose is not to rank, but to determine what students have learned and to help them improve if we feel they have not learned well enough.

SATs and GPAs are related in a very odd way. Milton, Pollio, and Eison (1986) studied the rise and fall of SAT scores and GPAs from 1950 to 1980. The findings were striking: When one goes up, the other goes down. There may be some debate about just what the SAT (or the ACT) measures, but whatever it is, when student performance on the SAT goes down, GPAs have gone up, and when student performance on the SAT has gone up, GPAs have gone down. By SAT standards, better students at one historical moment are being graded more stringently than weaker students at another historical moment. Thus, the relationship between what the SAT measures and GPAs is not what is usually assumed to be the case. Moreover, the value of the grades that make up a student's GPA is not standard across historical periods. Once again it is apparent that grades are meaningful only in the immediate context in which they are given; grades are not an unequivocal set of symbols that bear absolute meanings when stripped of contextual factors. It also appears that grade contexts are shaped not only by the values and practices of individual instructors and students but also by qualities of the larger historical era in which grades are given.

Faculty, students, parents, and business people do not agree on what grades "really" mean. In their national survey of attitudes toward grades, Milton, Pollio, and Eison (1986) designed several questions to determine what grades meant to students, faculty, parents, and potential employers. While there were areas of agreement across groups, there were also some striking areas of disagreement. For example, when asked how long they thought the difference between an A and a C would last, 53% of faculty members felt it would last from two to five years or longer; only 14% of students felt this way. Of the students, however, 45% felt any difference between an A and a C was simply non-existent or would last at most for three months; only 14% of faculty members agreed with this opinion. The duration of whatever a grade measures is simply not apparent to many students, even when they regard the grade as an important token.

Parents' and business respondents' opinions about grades also differed from those of students and faculty. In regard to how long the differences between an A and a C would last, 34% of parents and only 19% of business respondents felt that such differences were non-existent or would last less than three months. When we look at the other end of the scale and compare values for the view that A-C differences last two to four years or longer, results revealed that 33% of parents and 32% of business respondents reported this as their belief. These additional results suggest that to those who received good grades in their own student days — college instructors — grades appear to convey significant and long-lasting information about the abilities of the students to whom they are assigned. Parents and business respondents are somewhat more sanguine than current students about grades, but they also tend to view grades as less significant than college professors do. Whatever else this may suggest, it indicates all too often that faculty and students are giving and receiving symbols about whose significance they disagree markedly. The same difference in perception also applies to the two major users of the symbols: business people and parents.

The older generation — faculty, parents, and business recruiters — did agree on one issue: their belief that grades predict future success. For these three groups, 37%, 39%, and 35% checked the categories of "high" or "very high" in describing their views of the relationship between college grades and future success in life. The comparable value for students was 25%, again suggesting that students see much less value in grades than others do.

We have argued that grades should be viewed as addressed essentially to students within the specific context of an individual classroom and course — indeed, the results of the national grade survey found that faculty and students agree this should be the primary use of grades — but all groups also recognize that grades are addressed to and used by others. It is therefore striking that while 80% of business recruiters look at the GPA, over 70% of companies that have minimum cutoff scores use 2.75 (or less) as their value. Given the ambiguities that surround the GPA, such a low cutoff seems wise. Only 11% of business recruiters report that their companies have conducted any studies evaluating the predictive value of grades. It almost appears as if the use of the GPA in decisions made by business recruiters reflects a ritualistic legacy, a homage to semisacred symbols whose import is lost in ambiguity. While 38% of business recruiters say grades are of "great" importance for initial hiring, only 16% say grades determine initial salary or selection for special training programs, and only 2% consider grades of "great" importance for subsequent promotions.

To link this result with selection procedures used to admit students to graduate school, faculty and business recruiters were asked to rank-order several criteria for selecting graduate students or employees. Although both faculty and recruiters viewed grades in major courses as one major criterion for selection, the remaining criteria that both groups considered of great significance were different. Graduate-selection faculty deemed the following items crucial: number of difficult courses completed, breadth of courses taken, scores on standardized tests, and samples of student writing. For business, the following items were considered most important: nature of non-college jobs held, student personality, and participation in extracurricular activities. It seems clear that business recruiters consider a lot of non-academic factors in selecting employees.

There is not much correlation between grades and future success in life. Responses on the degree to which grades are believed to predict future success were different for student and faculty groups. Students saw grades as having little predictive potential for future success (21% saw them as of little or no use, and 25% saw them as highly useful), while faculty saw them as having good predictive potential (only 10% saw them as having no use, and 37% saw them as highly useful). Results of a host of correlational analyses reveal that students are closer to the mark than their "markers" are. At least four major reviews (Hoyt, 1965; Nelson, 1975; Cohen, 1984; Baird, 1985) point to the same conclusion: The data do not support the common faculty view, and this is bound to be surprising to most faculty members. A basic result yielded by these surveys — and these were not undertaken by avowed opponents to grades and to the GPA, but either by neutral observers (Hoyt, Nelson, Cohen) or by Baird (who had a fellowship at Educational Testing Service when he wrote the review) — was that in no case was the average correlation between GPA and adult achievement (however measured) higher than .20, although it did drop as low as .09. The general range of values, based on a 95% confidence interval, never went higher than .31 and got as low as -.03. The overall conclusion must be that when a great many correlations produced by a great many different individuals, at many different time periods and involving a great many different criteria, are examined together, correlations between GPAs and future achievement are just not impressive. Although there are some statistical problems involved in interpreting the meaning of these correlations (for example, most correlations deal with a restricted range of grade scores, a situation that reduces correlations), the overall conclusion must be that grades do not do a very good job of predicting future adjustment or success.

Parents react in predictable ways to good and bad grades. As might be expected, how frequently parents react to both good and bad grades changes from elementary school through college. What may be surprising, however, is that reactions to grades show little or no association with good grades, and that certain reactions to bad grades actually show a negative relationship (Milton, Pollio, and Eison, 1986; Pollio, Humphreys, and Milton, 1987). There are complex problems involved in providing an unequivocal (or any) interpretation for the negative correlations observed between parental reactions and grades. The best interpretation seems to be that parents get angry at poor grades across all levels of the educational system, and this reaction does nothing to change things; if anything, it keeps things going in the same direction. Parental reactions neither cause nor ameliorate bad grades; they simply co-vary with them. There may well be important psychological reasons for parental reactions to grades, and a family's valuation of grades clearly plays a significant role in shaping a child's attitudes toward them. In terms of altering the grades a student receives, however, parental reactions are at best insignificant and possibly even detrimental to improving grades. Grading remains rooted in the individual classroom.

An analysis of parental reactions to both good and bad grades reveals that bad grades provoke many parents to sarcasm or anger, whereas good grades spark pride and rewards. One possible reason for these powerful reactions is that grades are viewed not only as an evaluation of academic performance but also, and more important, as a measure of one's adequacy as a parent or as indicating that one's child might not be smart enough, hardworking enough, or able to cope with personal stress. Parents worry about the future success of their children, and the meanings usually associated with grades cut a wide path across basic aspects of being a "good" parent and of having a "good" child. Parental reactions seem more pertinent to the needs of parents than to those of students or of teaching and learning.

Attention to the use made of grades by business recruiters and to parental reactions simply reinforces the fundamental observation that grades, primarily and essentially, must be used as a mode of communication between teachers and students in the specific learning situations defined by distinct courses. The proper context for grades is also the basic context for learning; grades thus should be employed in ways that facilitate significant learning, as suggested in the following recommendations.

Recommendations

Most faculty are averse to tilting at windmills, and most perceive grades and grading (and GPAs) as so ingrained in university life that little can be done to correct abuses. Yet we also believe that some things can be done to improve the legitimate use of grades and grading in a specific classroom as a communication between teacher and student, so as to facilitate teaching and learning. Sustained and thoughtful faculty discussion of grading in relation to testing and course requirements is important — but not to bring uniformity to our practices or to coerce colleagues into procedures antithetical to their values. Rather, attention to these issues brings greater clarity to classroom values and procedures; suggests new approaches to grading, teaching, learning, and testing; and promotes a greater collegial understanding of these matters as students experience them in specific individual classes.

The context in which grades are meaningfully given, received, and used is the individual course or class. Within this context, grades are best used as a communication between an instructor and a student. When we perceive grades as part of a complex process of communication, we recognize that they can be used to facilitate learning. Faculty should clarify, individually and collegially, their understanding of grades, with this as their primary emphasis. They should not encourage the use too often made of these symbols: to rank and sort students for other institutional and societal purposes.

Instructors should integrate the basic criteria and procedures for grading into their approaches to teaching and learning. Grading should flow from course objectives and instructional strategies, not vice versa. An instructor's grading system and procedures should be coherent and, above all, apparent to the student from the outset of a course. This is not simply to allow students enmeshed in the grading game to escape being caught off base and tagged out, but to ensure that the terms of communication are clear and their relevance to what will be asked of students apparent. Grading procedures, and the tests and assignments on which they are based, must be tied to some overall logic of the course and the instructional strategies designed to implement it. If the instructor wants to promote higher orders of critical and creative thinking, and if the necessary risk-taking that goes with such activities is valued, then tests and course requirements must allow and even demand these activities.

Since grades are based on classroom tests, special attention should be given to improving tests. Our tests define our academic values in ways that transcend all that we say in our opening monologues or in our course syllabi. Improving tests entails reflection, practice, and skill, as well as critiques by colleagues at times, especially if we are to design questions and activities that involve students in higher levels of critical and creative thinking. Feedback to students on tests and other assignments should contain more than the simple notation of a grade or indications of what is right or wrong. A test is not only a grading device, but also a teaching technique in its own right (Milton, 1982).

We must recognize that grades are judgments made by human beings about complex processes. As judgments, they are necessarily subjective. This does not mean that they are capricious or arbitrary; it does mean that they are made in specific contexts, and that these contexts are shaped by a number of factors, ranging from the social characteristics and values of a specific historical era to the priorities and perceptions of individual students and teachers. Grades are human judgments about a complex human phenomenon; they cannot always be quantified or expressed with the exacting precision of a number taken to the second decimal. As grades, we must not idolize numerical quantification, nor should we reify too-fine distinctions not supported by the evidence on which they are supposedly based.

Each instructor should consider the number of units used in the grading scale. Just because institutions allow a five-, thirteen-, or hundred-unit scale does not mean we must use all categories on the scale. If our concern is to communicate to students our perceptions of what they know, rather than to place them in rank order, then fewer units may well serve most faculty. The grading scale should be no more finely calibrated than the information that shapes an instructor's judgments about student learning will allow.

Criteria and procedures should be fairly applied. It is striking how often students cite matters of grading as examples of unfair treatment. Nowhere is the power that resides in the hands of faculty so apparent, or so open to abuse. Some problems may be based in misperceptions of just what factors count in the eyes of a given instructor. Whether and how often one is willing to take account of so-called extraneous factors in determining grades is a matter for each instructor to decide, both in his or her own mind and in communication with students. If late papers simply will not be accepted or always will receive a penalty, this policy should be specified, for students have other instructors whose policies are different. It should go without saying — yet student anecdotal evidence indicates that this is not always the case — that factors such as gender and race must not enter into grading.

If our emphasis is helping students learn and demonstrate learning, we can avoid grading on a curve. To treat each class as a clear sample of some whole, and to accept the task of ranking and sorting as central to the classroom, forces instructors to assume adversarial positions against students and to distort testing and other evaluation procedures. We can recognize that all are not equally gifted and still make a fundamental attempt to bring all students in a class to certifiable levels of mastery. This is not a call for awarding all students A's; we simply suggest recognizing that each class is a complex entity, and assessment within it need not genuflect to external institutional and societal needs.

Faculty should seek appropriate information and avoid absolutizing grades. Faculty members often serve on all sorts of committees that make judgments about students on the basis of academic records for admission to college, specific programs, graduate and professional school; for financial aid; for academic probation or honors; and for other ends. In so doing, faculty should avoid taking out of context and removing the factors that provided their meaning. Above all, we should be wary of the GPA — a falsely precise statistic that launders grades by removing all contextual meaning, reifies grades by attributing to them properties they cannot have, and absolutizes grades by assuming they convey clear and uniform meanings. Decisions about admissions, financial aid, progress, and honors must be made, and faculty should play a significant role in making them. Therefore, we must give careful thought to the basis on which we make these decisions. We must not allow our reflections on grading and our uses of grades to be governed by sorting and ranking procedures, which are all too often at odds with grades as tools to facilitate teaching and learning through effective communication between instructors and students. We must learn to make judgments and stop relying on the GPA to take the responsibility for such judgments out of our hands.

References

Baird, L.L. "Do Grades and Tests Predict Adult Accomplishment?" *Research in Higher Education,* 23 (1985): 3-85.

Balch, J. "The Influence of the Evaluating Instruments on Students' Learning." *American Educational Research Journal,* 1 (1964): 169-182.

Barnett, D.C., & Dalton, J. "Why College Students Cheat." *Journal of College Student Personnel,* 22 (1981): 545-551.

Class, E. "The Effect of the Kind of Test Announced on Students' Preparation." *Journal of Educational Research* 28 (1935): 358-361.

Cohen, P.A. "College Grades and Adult Achievement." *Research in Higher Education,* 20 (1984): 281-293.

Eison, J.A.; Pollio, H.R.; & Cunningham, P. "Testing Preferences of Learning- and Grade-Oriented University Students." *Teaching of Psychology.* In press.

Eison, J.A.; Pollio, H.R.; & Milton, O. "Educational and Personal Characteristics of Four Different Types of Learning- and Grade-Oriented Students." *Contemporary Educational Psychology,* 11 (1986): 54-67.

Hakstian, R. "The Effects of Type of Examination Anticipated on Test Preparation and Performance." *Journal of Educational Research,* 64 (1971): 319-324.

Hoyt, D.P. *The Relationship Between College Grades and Adult Achievement: A Review of the Literature.* ACT Research Report 7. Iowa City, IA: American College Testing Program, 1965.

Milton, O. *Will That Be on the Final?* Springfield, IL.: Thomas, 1982.

Milton, O.; Pollio, H.R.; & Eison. J.A. *Making Sense of College Grades: Why the Grading System Does Not Work and What Can Be Done About It.* San Francisco: Jossey-Bass, 1986.

Nelson, A.M. *Undergraduate Academic Achievement as an Indication of Success.* Washington, DC: Civil Service Commission Report, 1975.

Pollio, H.R. "What Students Think About and Do in College Lecture Classes." *Teaching-Learning Issues,* 53 (1984): 3-18.

Pollio, H.R.; Humphreys, W.L.; & Milton, O. *Components of Contemporary Grade Meanings.* Technical Report No. 4. Learning Research Center, University of Tennessee, Knoxville, 1987.

Examinations: Accentuating the Positive

Miriam McMullen-Pastrick and Maryellen Gleason

Instructors today are well aware of the importance ascribed to grades — by society and by students. Institutions of almost every sort use grades as part of the admissions criteria. Furthermore, grade point averages are gatekeepers to a number of professions. Students learn the significance of grades early and before long justifiably conclude that grades signify more than mastery of content. Unfortunately, their next conclusion is that grades objectively measure intelligence and self-worth. When exams are returned, their conclusion about intelligence is intensified, and it is aggravated by their susceptibility to peer pressure. As graded exams are distributed, the anything but idle query "Whadija get?" echoes around the room, and failure becomes a matter of public record.

Instructors know all this; their experiences with students provide repeated confirmation. What instructors know less well is the impact their communication strategies and techniques have on student exam experiences. This paper proposes to show how constructive communication can alter and positively affect student attitudes so that *learning* objectives for testing can be reclaimed and grades and their averages put into a more proper perspective. To accomplish these objectives, communication with students about exams is necessary at the beginning of the course, before each test, on the test itself, and when results are returned.

A Philosophy of Testing

Before saying anything to students about exams, instructors ought to review their own beliefs about the evaluation process. Unfortunately, the attitudes of students, parents, other educators, and society generally can infect an individual instructor. Knowing what one personally believes about exam objectives and results can provide guidelines for subsequent interactions with students.

During the planning of the syllabus, care and thought need to be directed to what style of learning evaluation will best allow each student to demonstrate individual ability to manipulate the important concepts of a particular body of knowledge. Then, whether convenient or inconvenient, simple or complex, this method should be implemented.

Philosophies of evaluation are legion, and the right to make individual choices on how to test learning is regarded as sacrosanct. Prevailing attitudes about the importance of grades cloud fundamental issues that deserve to be reviewed in adopting an exam philosophy. For example, exam results say nothing about the value or dignity of the individual. Single (or even multiple) exam scores do not justify comprehensive conclusions about an individual student's inherent intellectual ability or lack of it. Moreover, the first (or even the second) grade in a course does not determine student success in the whole course, let alone in life. All that can be said for most exams is just that they attempt to measure, at a particular juncture in time, a student's ability to demonstrate mastery of some information and some skills. Put another way, exams are not the solitary apex of academic life.

Furthermore, the ways that exams can be used to *promote* — and not simply to *assess* — learning ought to be reviewed. Ebel, in a now classic chapter, identifies four learning objectives that exams can accomplish:

1) to stimulate teachers to clarify objectives,

2) to motivate students,

3) to direct efforts of teachers and students toward attainment of essential achievements, and

4) to provide effective learning exercises (Ebel, 1958, p.52).

His point that exams can promote learning implies that they do not automatically accomplish this aim. The point is especially worth making today when the purpose of exams, grades, and evaluation is often distorted by the current use that society makes of them.

With a philosophy of exams and a set of objectives in mind, an instructor's next task is to communicate the essence of both. The best time for putting exams into the perceptual framework of the course is when the class begins. Students *want* to know the essentials: how many exams, when, how much do they count, and how grades are computed. Students *need* to know more: what the instructor believes about exams, what s/he hopes they will accomplish, and what s/he takes the grades to mean. This information helps students put exams in the larger context of course goals, seeing them as one of a variety of ways they will interact with course content. The content of the discussion ought to convey that, while exams are important and to be taken seriously, other aspects of the course have status as well.

Communicating Appropriate Expectations

During the time before an exam, instructors ought to be communicating about its content. Although it is tempting on a sunny afternoon when minds are wandering to reclaim attention with the comment, "For the next exam you will need to know ...," such a pronouncement ought to be avoided. It implies that course information is something to be learned for the exam but not for anything else. And, as a consequence, some day in class an instructor will labor to explain a complexity, struggle with examples and applications, and patiently probe to ensure comprehension, only to be asked at the conclusion, "Do we need to know this for the next exam?"

On the other hand, students should not be left in doubt about what they need to know for the next exam. The relative importance of the course content needs to be stated routinely.

- All course content is important, but what is essential?

- What fundamental facts drive the rest?

- What concepts inform the practice?

These are the questions instructors need to answer as part of their preparation for class and before their preparation of exams. Such queries can help assure teachers that they have dealt successfully with those questions if, at the conclusion of each class session, they pose a query like, "If you had to create a test question from what we've discussed in class today, what would you ask?" The ensuing discussion can show whether the important ideas came across, as well as summarize the session. Moreover, the discussion might generate an exam item.

Review sessions with students ought not to be billed as interactions when we "talk about what is going to be on the next exam." Rather, they should be described as exploratory exchanges during which both instructor and student share perceptions of relative content importance. Let students set the agenda. Announce that 45 minutes of the period preceding the exam will be set aside for review. Ask students to identify the content areas that they would like to discuss.

Students should come to tests with a clear set of content expectations and, in addition, they will do better if they have a clear understanding of the exam format. Are the questions to be multiple-choice, true-false, matching, fill-in, short answer, essay, or are they to be a combination? Sample questions will give a flavor of the instructor's test writing style. How much time will be allowed to complete the exam? Will the sections of the test be weighted differently?

Two arguments make a strong case for communicating information about exam structure. First, the goal is to evaluate students' interaction with the *content*, not the *format*, of the exam. Knowing the format permits that focus and in the process alleviates one source of anxiety. Second, sharing accurate information about exams diminishes the adversarial aspects of the teacher-student relationship where all too often the perception is that one party is out to get the other, and the place to do it is on the exams. Instructors can talk about tests without "giving away what's on the exam." For example, exam objectives can be reiterated: "I'm hoping from this experience you will learn how to ...." Explaining how the exam facilitates the accomplishment of learning goals helps students build accurate exam expectations.

The Instructor's Response

Feedback is the process that guarantees message integrity. It permits the instructor to communicate with individual students about whether they have properly understood the content they received. Research indicates that instructor response is most effective when it is given promptly, includes information about what is right as well as wrong, and is clearly understood (Barnlund, 1968).

It follows that exams ought to be graded promptly and that excellent answers and/or sections ought to be identified as often as deficient ones. If an exam is generally poor, identifying the one or two good answers can provide essential encouragement and prevent an overwhelming sense of failure. Finally, instructor response must be accurately interpreted, which may mean something as simple as a teacher's having legible writing. It takes time to make comments on exams but that time is wasted if students cannot read the written remarks.

In addition, instructors' remarks need to make some sort of sense standing alone. All too often students quickly leaf through a returned exam reading only the instructor's comments without reviewing what they themselves wrote. Wise instructors will reckon with that practice as they write their comments about students' answers. Finally, instructors' comments ought to appear in the margin or other empty space and not be superimposed on student writing. The practice of writing over what students have said discourages them from re-reading their own work and may be taken as a sign that the teacher lacks respect for their ideas.

Large class sizes have seemed to necessitate the move to machine-scored exams. The convenience cannot be argued. Means, deviations, and item analyses can be circulated upon request. What the computer printouts cannot pinpoint, however, is the cause of error: 75% of the class missed question 13, but data do not say why. Sometimes looking at actual tests may provide clues, especially in the case of questions requiring problem-solving. Moreover, instructor comments, even isolated ones, can communicate personal concern. Instructors who use machine scoring should consider the possibility of hand-grading some of each set of exams in order to find out the details of how students are responding and to provide at least some personal feedback.

Instructors also ought to be aware of the messages implicit in the marks made on exams. For example, in essay answers, instructors may underline key words or phrases as they read along. Unfortunately, this practice reinforces the student perception that success stems from the use of certain pivotal terms or phrases and not from how the essay is ordered or what is said about those key words.

Not only is it important that instructors give feedback on exams, it is equally important that they receive feedback. Some of that response is inherent in student answers, but it can be solicited as well. A brief exam evaluation, like the one shown in figure 1, can be attached to the test. It might ask questions like:

- Did the content you expected to see appear on this exam?

- Were you clear as to what the questions were asking? (List the number(s) of the question(s) that you were unclear about.)

- Are you satisfied with your response to most of the test questions?

Conclude the evaluation with a space for students to assign a grade *to the exam* and to add comments. Not only does this strategy provide the instructor with response about the exam itself, it reinforces the idea that instructor and student are jointly engaged in learning. Finally this practice gives the students the opportunity, for once, to *give* grades and not just *receive* them.

Returning the Results

Given the importance ascribed to exams and the anxiety inherent in having to demonstrate content mastery, it is no wonder that the real rhetorical challenge confronts the instructor on the day that the exam results are returned. It is also not surprising that some teachers opt to avoid this encounter. For example, some teachers post the scores and refuse to take class time to discuss them. This strategy is barely bettered by the one in which exams are passed out in the last five minutes and all of 30 seconds are offered to entertain comments. On the other hand, there is the brave instructor who actually discusses the exam in class, but stands firm in the face of any and every student objection — sometimes appearing in the process rigid, autocratic, and occasionally stupid. Another stance finds the instructor caving into student objections and giving away points as if the whole testing process had no validity.

The major key to a successful handling of exam results is simple: prepare. Before taking exam results to a class, determine what ought to be said about them. These decisions should be informed by a larger sense of objectives for the discussions of exams. What should be accomplished during a period when exams are returned? For example, a classroom review of results can focus on what was learned — a question to be raised with students directly — or discussions can provide summaries of content segments and help make the transition to new areas. They can be used to identify areas of misunderstanding and lead to clarification. If a large percentage of students has missed a particular question, and the instructor determines that the question fairly represents the content, a defense (as in justification or rationale) ought to be considered. Such discussions can lead to a consideration of study strategies, helping students to identify productive ways of managing course content.

In all these examples, the discussion can reinforce the central point that exams serve more purposes than the generation of grades.

Student Evaluation of Exam

A. Please respond to the following questions by writing YES or NO on the line at the end of the question:

1. Did the content you expected to see appear on this exam? .... 1. ____
2. Were you clear as to what the questions were asking? .... 2. ____
3. List the number(s) of the question(s) that you were unclear about. .... 3. ____
4. Are you satisfied with your response to most of the test questions? .... 4. ____
5. List the number(s) of the question(s) for which you were not satisfied with your response. .... 5. ____

B. Assign a percentage grade on the line after the following statements. The grade should reflect how well you believe the test accomplished each objective.

1. Exam corresponded to text content. .... 1. ____
2. Exam corresponded to class lectures. .... 2. ____
3. Exam related to class discussions. .... 3. ____
4. Exam challenged you to think creatively. .... 4. ____
5. Exam included concepts studied in homework assignments. .... 5. ____
6. Exam motivated you to question ideas you previously took for granted. .... 6. ____

C.
1. Which part of the test most challenged your thinking? Explain.
2. Which part of the exam least challenged your thinking? Explain.
3. If you were to take this exam again with only one section remaining the same, what section would it be? Explain why.
4. If you were to take this test again and only one section could be changed, what section would you choose? Explain your choice.

D.
1. Grade the exam. That is, assign the test a letter grade based on its form, content, and fairness.
2. How well do you think you did on the exam? That is, guess how many of the possible points you will receive.

Figure 1

Students' Objections

A variety of strategies can be used in dealing with students' objections. The first is to respond with a non-defensive description of why the question is legitimate and a certain answer is correct. If student objections persist and appear to gain converts among other class members (who convert easily, especially if they, too, missed the item), broaden the discussion to include others, forcing a variety of persons to make the point. If the argument has legitimacy, a few strategies can prevent the appearance of caving into student pressure.

Defer the decision. Tell students that lecture notes, text material, and possibly other sources need to be consulted and that a decision will be made and explained further in the next class. This delay provides an opportunity for reflection. When the decision is made, it ought not to be subject to further discussion.

Another strategy is to offer students an opportunity to write out their objections. Credit alterations can be made on the merit of each individual case, so that the points are not given wholesale to lucky guessers who gain additional points because of another student's argument. The same tack might be taken with students who are generally upset with the whole exam. Encourage them to rewrite the exam, including the content they expected to appear on this test. The results of this activity may legitimately merit some exam score alteration.

The communication style and psychological stance of the instructor during the discussion of the exam results are also crucial determinants for making the processing of the exam a valid learning experience. Jack Gibb provides a schema for recognizing communication behaviors in terms of being defensive or supportive (Gibb, 1961), and Joseph DeVito augments the application of the Gibb communication climates (DeVito, 1986). To create a communication environment that is supportive of students' efforts, discussions of exam results need to favor *description* over *evaluation*. If students perceive that the intent is to provide them with data that is supportive of their learning process, (Bergquist and Phillips, 1975) then they will hear the discussion and benefit from the exchange. If, however, students sense that the occasion is judgmental in focus, they will be alienated.

The teacher clearly has a powerful position, and evaluation often tends to create tension and defensiveness in those being evaluated. To counterbalance these dynamics, discussions of exam results ought to be kept descriptive as opposed to evaluative (DeVito, 1986). Avoid judgmental assessments like, "You misunderstood the question." Describe what the student ought to have done. "Read the question in terms of the context in which your text presents it and think about the points made in class discussion; these should provide you with a clearer understanding of how to focus your answer." Exams by their nature pass enough judgment, and instructors' comments need not make them even more judgmental.

In the classroom processing of exam results, the instructor needs a psychological stance of openness and spontaneity, and these qualities of pedagogical integrity cannot be feigned. Instructor responses which are genuine and appropriate to the topic under discussion create a supportive environment. A student/instructor exchange, which demonstrates that the instructor honors the possibility of alternatives, frees students to share some of their sophisticated reasoning processes. Usually students are willing to risk such insights only in a very trust-filled environment. Only an open-minded teacher can generate such a classroom atmosphere.

There is no magic formula for alleviating all the stress that surrounds exams, nor is there a panacea for satisfying everyone in each test. But, careful and sensitive planning, preparation, and processing of exams can make them a vital part of teaching and learning. Attending to communication details can, in addition, put exams and grades in a perspective consistent with the proper aims of education.

References

Barnlund, Dean C. *Interpersonal Communication: Survey and Studies*. Boston: Houghton Mifflin, 1968. Pp. 229-231.

Bergquist, William H., & Phillips, Steven R. "Characteristics of Constructive Feedback." In *A Handbook for Faculty Development*. Council for Advancement of Small Colleges, 1975. Pp. 224-225.

DeVito, Joseph. *The Interpersonal Communication Book*. New York: Harper and Row, 1986. Pp. 68-81.

Ebel, Robert L. "Using Examinations to Promote Learning." In Cooper, Russell M., ed., *The Two Ends of the Log*, 52. Minneapolis: University of Minnesota Press, 1958.

Gibb, Jack R. "Defensive Communication," *Journal of Communication* 11 (September 1961): 141-148.

Lowman, J. *Mastering the Techniques of Teaching*. San Francisco: Jossey-Bass, 1984.

McCormick-Scott, Ann. "Life is a Multiple-Choice Question." *AHA Perspective*, December 1986: 16-18.

Exam Review Sessions

Maryellen Weimer

"Are you going to spend time reviewing for the exam?" students frequently query instructors. Sometimes the question is more blatant: "Are you going over what's going to be on the exam?" Students do not expect to be told what the exam items are, but they're hoping to discover as many details as they can possibly squeeze out of the instructor.

This kind of student pressure causes many faculty members to wonder about the value and purpose of exam review sessions. Should they be incorporated into already crowded course calendars? Do students perform better on exams if instructors include review sessions? More important, do review sessions contribute to the long-term retention of course content? Do sessions like these help students better cope with exam anxiety? How can the sessions be formatted? What about mechanics — like time, attendance, participation of TAs, and so on?

The case for offering review sessions rests on two principal arguments: The sessions do contribute to the learning potential of exams, and they do help students cope with exam anxiety.

In the first case, review sessions help students better learn the content by creating accurate expectations about how knowledge of the content will need to be demonstrated, and how detailed that knowledge needs to be. The sessions can be designed to give students an opportunity to practice the skills needed on the exam.

Helping students cope with exam anxiety is equally important. Some students feel so much anxiety that their performance on the exam suffers. They know the content, they can solve the problems, but the pressure of the situation prevents them from demonstrating that knowledge. Instructors point out that students must learn to cope with anxiety, to perform under pressure — but few can point to jobs in the "real" world that require students to perform under college examination conditions. The process of reviewing under an instructor's guidance, with his encouragement, bolsters students' confidence. Information about exam logistics, like the number and format of the questions, helps them relax and concentrate on content.

As far as empirical evidence is concerned, the effects of review sessions on learning outcomes does not rank as one of the well-researched topics in higher education. However, instructors who monitor student participation in review sessions and scores on exams report a positive correlation between the two.

In fact, one faculty member we know significantly increases attendance at the review session for the second exam by posting on the board the average score of students who attended the first exam review next to the average for those who didn't. He reports the average of those attending has never failed to be higher. He does grudgingly admit that the difference may not result from the review session as much as from student ability (we all know who attends voluntary review sessions), but even so the difference serves to motivate a number of students, and that's his objective.

Ways to Go

As for format, instructors use a variety of them, but consider these three fairly common approaches:

The first might be called the *open question period*. Here the instructor simply makes himself available to the students; they set the agenda. They decide what questions to ask, what problems they'd like solved, or what parts of the reading they want reviewed. If they ask questions for only five minutes, so be it, and the review session ends.

This approach does give students the opportunity to clarify those parts of the content they don't understand. However, it fails to establish content priorities or focus. Frequently this approach lends itself to the "20 questions" routine, with students trying to weasel as much information from faculty as possible. The learning potential of the session diminishes to the degree students get into the mode of asking, "Do we have to know X for the exam?" "Will there be questions on X?"

Some instructors still try to provide students an open questioning arena, but focus questions, possibly even recasting some, by having students submit them prior to the review. Discussion of those questions takes precedence over questions students bring to — or that arise during — the review session itself.

Another approach attempts to simulate *actual exam experiences*. Students work on possible or previous exam problems or questions. The instructor may encourage them to discuss their solution with other students or check for the answer in lecture notes or text material. The instructor concludes by clarifying any still-unresolved questions about the answer. The success of these sessions depends on the degree to which students do the work. They learn something about how to solve a problem when they see an instructor do it, but they learn something much more relevant when they solve the problem themselves. Review sessions like these give instructors opportunities to help students plan their study time and develop some strategies to use during the exam.

The exam-experience sessions also permit the instructor to include some information on how exam items will be graded. Some teachers incorporate actual examples — using a sample short answer from a previous semester, or a problem solution derived by a group who have worked on the problem during the session. This helps students understand the process of grading as well as showing them what instructors look for in answers. Both experiences — answering actual exam questions and seeing answers graded — motivate and prepare students for what's to come.

Review sessions can also be used to *integrate content chunks*. Dhanraj Sahadeo and William E. Davis advocate this approach in an excellent article, "Review — Don't Repeat" (*College Teaching*, Summer 1988, p. 111): "The students come to the review focused on the 'parts'; they are concerned with the formulas, dates, theorems, pathways, problems, definitions and quotations they expected to be tested. In an integrative review, the instructor addresses these parts in a way that fits them all together, providing an overview of the whole now that the parts are known in detail."

This approach does help to prevent random and relentless student questioning. As a planned period of instruction, the teacher directs and paces the session. Students may ask questions, are encouraged to, but the questions now are part of a larger context. The instructor focuses, according to Sahadeo and Davis, on "how the course content was organized and why."

Certainly, review sessions may combine more than one of these approaches, as well as approaches not described here. There is no magic formula that results in the "best" review session. The details — including the mechanics of when to schedule the session, whether to require attendance, whether TAs should be in charge — need to fit the instructor's objectives, preparedness of the students, and nature of the content. Used intelligently, review sessions offer an instructional strategy that combines students' interest in grades with an interest in learning. The result? Better teaching.

Improving Multiple-Choice Tests

Victoria L. Clegg and William E. Cashin

"The tendency in course examinations is to pose the question 'How much do you remember of what has been covered?' rather than 'What can you do with what you have learned?' "
— Dressel (1976, p.208)

The classroom test is one of the most important aspects of the teaching-learning process, and designing the classroom test is one of the most demanding responsibilities facing college and university instructors. Unfortunately, most of us have had little, if any, preparation in the craft of writing tests. Consequently, the process is not only difficult; it is also frustrating and often ineffective.

Writing test questions will always be demanding, even for experienced instructors, but it will be less frustrating for those who know the techniques for writing specific types of items and have some guidelines for general test construction.

The multiple-choice item has been chosen as the focus of this paper for three reasons:

- They can be written to evaluate higher levels of learning, such as integrating material from several sources, critically evaluating data, contrasting and comparing information.

- They can be very useful for diagnostic purposes, for helping students see their strengths and weaknesses.

- They are often used in college and university classes; therefore, it is especially important that instructors write them well.

Although these strengths are shared by some other item types, the multiple-choice item is a powerful teaching-learning tool if the instructor has designed the item properly.

What Is a Multiple-Choice Item?

The multiple-choice item requires that students select the correct answer to a question from an array of alternative responses that are written by the instructor. All multiple-choice items have the same three elements:

- an *item stem* that presents the problem,

- the *correct or keyed option*, and

- several *distractor options*, incorrect alternatives that are likely to be plausible to the student who has not completely mastered the learning being tested.

Several variations of the standard multiple-choice item have been used in classroom tests. Some of these will be described later. Typically, multiple-choice items present the problem in one of two formats: the complete question, e.g., "What is the most frequently used type of test item in college-level examinations?" or the incomplete statement, e.g., "The most frequent type of test item used in college-level examinations is ...." The students are directed to select either the correct answer or the best answer from the list of options provided. In the *correct answer* form, the answer is correct beyond question or doubt, while the others are definitely incorrect. In the *best answer* version, more than one option may be appropriate in varying degrees; however, it is essential that the keyed or "best" response be the one that competent experts would agree upon.

It may appear to be fairly simple to construct items in the multiple-choice format. Actually, the formatting is simple; it is constructing a meaningful and worthwhile item that is so difficult and time-consuming. "An ingenious and talented item writer can construct multiple-choice items that require not only the recall of knowledge but also the use of skills of comprehension, interpretation, application, analysis, or synthesis to arrive at the keyed answer" (Thorndike and Hagen, 1969, p. 103). How many of us who teach at colleges and universities would describe ourselves as "ingenious and talented" while we struggle to write effective multiple-choice items? Wilbert J. McKeachie (1986, p. 91) has said that "... the greater your experience in their construction, the longer it takes per [multiple-choice] item to construct a reasonably fair, accurate, and inclusive question." In other words, as you get better, things may seem worse! We cannot promise you ingenuity and talent. We do hope to help you become a more competent and successful writer of multiple-choice items by sharing some of the guidelines that measurement experts and experienced instructors have recommended.

Many college teachers believe the myth that the multiple-choice question is only a superficial exercise — a multiple-guess — requiring little thought and less understanding from the student. It is true that many multiple-choice items are superficial, but that is the result of poor test craftsmanship and not an inherent limitation of the item type. A well-designed multiple-choice item can test high levels of student learning, including all six levels of Bloom's (1956) taxonomy of cognitive objectives:

LEVELS OF COGNITIVE LEARNING

Evaluation: judging by using self-produced criteria or established standards

Synthesis: combining ideas into a statement or product new to the learner

Analysis: separating ideas into component parts, examining relationships

Application: problem-solving or applying ideas in new situations

Comprehension: restating or reorganizing material to show understanding

Knowledge: simple recognition or recall of material

Some writers prefer fewer levels, e.g., understanding (combining knowledge and comprehension), application, and higher-order cognitive objectives (combining analysis, synthesis, and evaluation). (See Gronlund, 1985b, for a further treatment of levels of educational objectives.)

Strengths of Multiple-Choice Tests

Multiple choice items are often described as the most versatile of all item types, suitable to a wide range of instructional goals:

- They can be used to test *all levels of learning*, from knowledge to evaluation.

- They can assess the *ability to integrate information* from several sources.

- They are very useful for *diagnosing student difficulties* if the incorrect options are written to reveal common errors.

- They provide an *excellent basis for post-test discussion*, especially if the discussion includes why the *distractors* are *wrong* as well as why the *correct answers* are *right*.

Multiple-choice items also share many of the strengths of other selected response items, i.e., true-false, matching, etc.:

- They can provide a *more comprehensive sample* of subject material because more questions can be asked.

- They adapt to a *wide range of content and difficulty levels*.

- They require relatively *less student time to answer*.

- They can be *easily and accurately scored* by a person or machine.

Limitations of Multiple-Choice Tests

Of course, multiple-choice items also have disadvantages:

- They are *open to misinterpretation* by students who read more into questions than was intended.

- They may *appear too picky* to students, especially when the options are well-constructed.

- When written to assess higher levels of learning, they require significant intellectual effort both in reading and in answering, *causing some students to be anxious*.

In addition, multiple-choice items share the limitations of other selected-response items:

- They *deny demonstration of knowledge beyond the range of options provided*.

- They are *difficult to phrase* so that all students will have the same interpretation.

- They take *time and skill* to construct effectively.

- They are so easily constructed to assess basic factual knowledge that instructors *often fail to test higher levels of thinking*.

- They are *ill-suited to assess affective or attitudinal learning* because they are easily "faked."

- They *encourage guessing* — after all, one option is correct.

Recommendations

When Should Multiple-Choice Items Be Used?

Knowing the strengths and limitations of multiple-choice items can help instructors make better decisions about whether or not to use these items in particular testing situations. Use multiple-choice items for the following instructional goals:

1. When you wish to test the *breadth of student learning*. Multiple-choice items offer the opportunity to sample a greater breadth of learning than do questions that require a lot of student writing. Because they take considerably less time to answer, many more questions can be asked and so more content tested.

2. When you want to test a *variety of levels of learning*. Multiple-choice items are extraordinarily flexible in that they can be used to assess the full range of Bloom's taxonomy (1956). Do not discount multiple-choice when you want to evaluate abilities to think critically and solve problems effectively.

3. When you have *many students* who will be taking the test, then multiple-choice tests are very efficient. If the class is very small in size, it usually is not worth the time it will take to construct an effective set of multiple-choice items. Carefully consider whether other item types will serve your testing purposes.

4. When you have *time to construct the test items*. Remember that effective multiple-choice items, which assess more than basic factual knowledge, require a great deal of time and effort to construct. If you do not have the time, another type of test will be a wiser choice.

5. When *time is limited for scoring*, then selected-response items are often the better choice. While it may have taken an hour to construct a multiple-choice item, it will take less than a second to score it.

6. When it is not important to determine how well the student can *formulate a correct or acceptable answer*. The answers are definitely provided in multiple-choice items. Even if the question requires critical thinking skills, it may be possible for a student to get the answer right because of clues in the options or by guessing. When it is important for students to formulate their own answers, multiple-choice will not do.

Required Preconditions

Before considering specific suggestions for writing multiple-choice items, there are a combination of abilities that, according to Alexander G. Wesman (1971), are necessary to write successful test items:

7. You must have a *thorough mastery of the subject matter* being tested. You must not only understand the implications of the facts and principles of a particular field, but you must also be aware of common fallacies and misconceptions.

8. You must *develop and use a set of educational objectives* to clearly guide your efforts to help students learn. Unless you have carefully considered what you want students to learn, you will not be able to evaluate their progress with any accuracy. This means that you must develop a test plan or table of specifications to guide your item writing. For the vast majority of tests, a two-dimensional table is sufficient. On one dimension, list the areas and subunits of the content you wish to test. On the second dimension, list the various levels of learning you wish to test — for example, understanding, application, and higher-order cognitive objectives. You must also decide what proportion of the test you want to devote to each area of content and each level of learning. Finally, as you write the test items, you should keep a tally of how many items fall into each cell of your total plan to ensure that your test actually covers the learning as you originally intended.

Example:

Levels of Learning

Topics	Understanding	Application	Higher-Order
A	5%	10%	10%
B	5%	20%	10%
C	10%	20%	10%

According to this table of specifications, approximately 40% of the instruction time was spent on topics "B" and "C" at the application level and 20% at the higher-order level. The test should reflect that proportion. (See Gronlund, 1985a, or Mehrens and Lehman, 1984, for further treatment of tables of specification.)

9. *Know the students* who will be taking the test, in order to appropriately adjust the complexity and difficulty of the items. Sophomores in Introduction 101 may look the same semester after semester, but there are likely to be many differences in the educational backgrounds and intellectual abilities of the groups. Design your test so that the students can demonstrate their learning.

10. You must be a *master of written communication*, able to communicate with precision and simplicity and you must use language that the students understand.

Constructing Multiple-Choice Items

The following recommendations for constructing multiple-choice items reflect the collective experience and wisdom of many authors. These recommendations are written in chronological order. Several works are listed in the References and Further Readings section for those of you who wish to read more extensively.

11. *Spread the work across time.* It is unwise to wait until the night before an exam is scheduled to construct the test items. It is impossible to construct effective multiple-choice items in such a limited time. Not only do you need time to construct the items; you need an opportunity to review and revise. If you write a question or two after each class or on a weekly basis, the collection is more likely to be representative of your instruction.

12. *Use note cards for writing the items.* This makes it much easier to file according to your test plan, rearrange, rewrite, and discard items. Better yet, if you have access to a personal computer, use it.

13. Really concentrate on writing items to *evaluate higher levels of thinking.* Avoid the pitfall of writing items that test only memorization of basic factual knowledge. Many instructors (especially those who are writing the test questions just before the test) fall into this trap and pull their students in with them.

14. *Write the stem first.* The stem should present a single, definite problem as a question or incomplete statement. The problem should be one of significance in the course.

15. Concentrate on *evaluating student ability to understand, apply, analyze, synthesize, and evaluate.* It is difficult to write questions that evaluate these higher cognitive levels; but if critical thinking is what you want students to do, you will have to test for it. Students have a tendency to study "what will be on the test" and to study *only* what will be on the test.

16. *State the problem concisely, but completely.* What the student is to answer must be obvious, and the student should be able to discern the problem without reading all of the options. A direct question usually does this more clearly than an incomplete statement. There are times, however, when the question is just too convoluted or confusing for easy interpretation; then the incomplete statement may be preferable, or perhaps an item type other than multiple-choice is more appropriate.

17. Write the stem to *include all the information essential to determining the problem,* but omitting irrelevant material that merely serves as padding — unless the students' determination of what is relevant is part of what you want to test.

18. *Avoid unnecessary repetition in the options* by including as much of the item as possible in the stem. This is especially important when using the incomplete statement format. Forcing students to reread a phrase several times wastes time they could put to better use when taking a test.

19. State the problem or ask the question *in a positive form.* The use of negatives can be confusing to even the most intelligent reader, and anxious students often completely miss little words like "not."

On those rare occasions when you decide that you must use negatives, use **boldface**, underlining, or CAPITAL letters. Do **not** use double negatives, e.g., negatives in both the stem and the options.

20. *Write the correct or best response after writing the stem.* Be certain that the best response is indeed *best*, that is, would be acknowledged as best by authorities in the field. State this response *as briefly as possible*, and without ambiguities so that all knowledgeable students will read it with the same interpretation. Having colleagues or former students critique your questions for clarity before using them on a test can help to avoid such difficulties.

21. *Avoid making the correct option longer than the distractors.* Test-wise students are very aware of this fault and use this clue to choose the correct answer without knowing the correct answer. The emphasis on the keyed response being absolutely correct sometimes leads to wordiness, and instructors tend to spend much less time developing the distractors, which then tend to be shorter. Write the correct response and the distractors, and then compare the lengths. If correct answers are consistently longer (or shorter) as you write multiple-choice items, edit as necessary.

22. *Write the distractors after writing the correct option.* The effectiveness of multiple-choice items can be undermined by sloppy preparation of the incorrect options. Designing distractors is actually quite challenging because these options must be wrong, yet be plausible enough to attract the attention of students who do not know the material as well as they should.

23. *Make all distractors plausible responses.* Avoid writing poor alternatives just for the sake of having more options; they simply become throwaway options. The criterion is whether or not the distractors test a discrimination that is important; if not, do not use it. Once in a while, a ridiculous option can relieve some of the tension that pervades a testing situation, but only once in a great while.

24. *Be sure that the distractors use words that ought to be familiar to the students.* Using highly technical language or the vocabulary of experts, terms that have not been used in class, forces students to choose correct answers without knowing the meaning of one or more of the options. If the students were not expected to learn the terms, do not include them in the options.

25. *Write distractors that are distinct from each other.* If all the distractors are too much alike, the test-wise student will use this clue to eliminate the group of look-alikes in favor of the dissimilar, correct response. Similar distractors may also indicate that the question should not be presented in the multiple-choice format. Avoid alternatives that overlap or include each other. This error is likely to be distracting to students who read carefully and know the material well, which can result in the more knowledgeable student being penalized by the instructor's lack of item-writing skills.

26. *Critique for general errors in style and format.* Delete any irrelevant clues that could lead a student to select the correct answer or eliminate one or more of the wrong options without knowing the material. Measuring the test-wiseness of the students is not the intent of the test.

27. *Be careful in using specific determiners,* such as "all," "never," "always," or other all-inclusive terms that are more likely to be found in incorrect options. Similarly, qualifiers such as "usually," "sometimes," and "maybe" are more likely to be found in the keyed item. However, sometimes the content permits using absolute specific determiners correctly, and so can keep the test-wise student "honest," e.g., "The president of the United States must always be at least 35 years old" is correct.

28. *Avoid grammatical inconsistencies* between the stem and the options. These are very useful clues for the student who is competent in syntax.

29. *Use "none of the above" as an option with caution.* Some faculty believe that the option "none of the above" should never be used in a multiple-choice item. This belief is correct for a "best answer" type item. (Nor should options like "all of the above" or "both A and B" be used in "best answer" items.) However, for "correct answer" items, where there definitely is a correct answer, the option "none of the above" may serve a useful purpose, especially for items requiring mathematical calculations, or perhaps correct spelling or grammar in a language. Using "none of the above" can prevent correct answers because of guessing, or save students from spending an inordinate amount of time on a problem they cannot solve. To be effective, the option must occasionally be the keyed response; otherwise, the students will see it simply as a throwaway option.

30. *Check once more* to be certain that the correct options are not consistently longer than the alternatives.

31. *Arrange options in a logical order,* if one exists. Numerical answers should be placed in numerical order and dates put in chronological order. Sometimes alphabetizing the options is appropriate.

Organizing the Layout of the Entire Test

Once the individual multiple-choice items are written, you must decide how to organize the groups of items on the test. If you are using several types of items on your exam, be sure to group all of the multiple-choice items together, etc.

32. *List options on separate lines*, arranged in a vertical column to clearly distinguish each option from the others. Printing the responses in tandem or arranging them across the page may save paper, but the result is difficult to read. You should not be testing reading skills.

33. *Use capital letters for the response options* if the student is to write the letter to indicate the selected answer. The handwritten, lower case letters "a" and "d" or "c" and "e" can be difficult to distinguish when scoring.

34. *Check to see that the correct answers are distributed randomly* among the possible option positions. If you have had a tendency to choose one position over others, for example, "B," it may become apparent to the test-wise student who seeks out such clues. If necessary, it is easy to rearrange the order of the options to correct this problem.

Interpretive Exercises

Many teacher-made multiple-choice tests pose a series of separate, unrelated questions. In contrast to this, the *interpretive exercise* format presents a series of multiple-choice items *based on a common stimulus*. The stimulus can be written material, also tables, graphs, maps, pictures, audio- or videotapes, etc. Interpretive exercise items can then be written to assess a wide range of student abilities — for example: to recognize generalizations, assumptions, or inferences; to apply principles; or to interpret data or experimental findings. To achieve this, however, the material must be novel or new to the students, not something previously covered in class or found in the textbook.

In addition to the general advantages of multiple-choice items in testing higher level and complex materials, interpretive exercises minimize the influence of irrelevant information because they confine the data to be interpreted to the material presented. This makes such exercises more difficult to construct; and for written material (the most common form), it places heavy demands upon reading skills. Nevertheless, we believe the advantages of interpretive exercises warrant their increased use in college-level tests. (Gronlund, 1985a, has an entire chapter on the interpretive exercise which we strongly recommend for your consideration.)

Conclusions

We have focused this paper on multiple-choice items because we are convinced that they permit testing higher levels of learning which are appropriate to college but which often are not tested by teacher-made tests (including essay as well as selected response tests). We are not suggesting that other forms of selected response items, e.g., true-false and matching, are inappropriate, but we have omitted them because of space limitation. (Several standard textbooks in the References and Further Readings section give detailed suggestions for designing such items.) Nor are we suggesting that multiple-choice items should, or can, replace essay tests. What we are suggesting is that many teacher-made multiple-choice tests can be significantly improved. We hope that this paper will be of some help to readers in achieving that improvement.

References and Further Readings

Those references below which are followed by an asterisk are standard texts on educational measurement. Each has one or more chapters on multiple-choice and other selection items, as well as chapters on other aspects of testing and grading.

Bloom, B.S., et al. *Taxonomy of Educational Objectives: Cognitive Domain*. New York: David McKay, 1956.

Campbell, J.R. *In Touch with Students*. Columbia: Kelly Press, 1972.

Clegg, V.L., & Owens, R.E. *Tips for Writing Tests*. Manhattan, KS: Graduate Services and Publications, 1984.

Dressel, P.L. *Handbook of Academic Evaluation*. San Francisco: Jossey-Bass, 1976.

Ebel, R.L., & Frisbie, D.A. *Essentials of Educational Measurement*. 4th ed. Englewood Cliffs, NJ: Prentice-Hall, 1986. *

Eble, K.E. *The Craft of Teaching: A Guide to Mastering the Professor's Art*. San Francisco: Jossey-Bass, 1976.

Educational Testing Service. *Multiple Choice Questions: A Closer Look*. Princeton, NJ: Author, 1973.

Fuhrmann, B.S., & Grasha, A.F. *A Practical Handbook for College Teachers*. Boston: Little, Brown, 1983.

Gronlund, N.E. *Measurement and Evaluation in Teaching*. 5th ed. New York: Macmillan, 1985a. *

Gronlund, N.E. *Stating Objectives for Classroom Instruction*. 3rd ed. New York: Macmillan, 1985b.

Lowman, J. *Mastering the Techniques of Teaching*. San Francisco: Jossey-Bass, 1984.

McKeachie, W.J. *Teaching Tips: A Guidebook for the Beginning Teacher*. 8th ed. Lexington, MA: D.C. Heath, 1986.

Mehrens, W.A., & Lehmann, I.J. *Measurement and Evaluation in Education and Psychology*. 3rd ed. New York: Holt, Rinehart and Winston, 1984. *

Milton, O. *Will That Be on the Final?* Springfield, IL: Charles C. Thomas, 1982.

Milton, O., & Associates. *On College Teaching: A Guide to Contemporary Practices*. San Francisco: Jossey-Bass, 1978.

Roid, G.H., & Haladyna, T.M. *A Technology for Test-Item Writing*. New York: Academic Press, 1982.

Thorndike, R.L., & Hagen, E. *Measurement and Evaluation in Psychology and Education*. New York: Wiley & Sons, 1969.

Wesman, A.G. *Writing the Test Item*. In Thorndike, R.L., ed., *Educational Measurement*. Washington, DC: American Council on Education, 1971.

Assessing Classroom Participation

Paul R. Lyons

Structured classroom discussions are increasingly popular with faculty members and students (Clarke, 1985; Wood, 1979; Armstrong and Boud, 1983). The emphasis on discussion comes from an increasing interest in student-centered approaches to teaching and learning. The valid, objective assessment of student participation in discussions presents many challenges for college faculty members, and this article suggests an approach that may help the faculty better evaluate and motivate student performance.

In many college courses, particularly upper-division undergraduate and lower-level graduate courses, class participation is often considered very important. It is not unusual to discover courses in which class participation performance is valued as 20% to 50% of the final course grade. Even with increased assessment of class participation, there has been very little written about it. Much of what has been written is of a descriptive nature, with an instructor-centered rating system applied during discussion or at some later time (Grieve, 1975; Clarke, 1985; Fisher, 1975). If class participation is intended to be significant, it is important to discover meaningful, timely, and relevant assessment methods.

Problems and Issues

Most college faculty members would agree that objective assessment of class participation is desirable. Perhaps a good deal fewer would agree on the likelihood of achieving objectivity. A teacher's personal likes and dislikes can influence the judgment of a student's performance.

Further, grading of discussion participation may increase student anxiety, which, in turn, may inhibit discussion. Knowing that they are being graded can place considerable pressure on students to participate in what they perceive to be a somewhat threatening environment.

The establishment of criteria for the assessment and evaluation of students' work is a most important factor in defining the performance that is expected and desired. Criteria can be expressed with varying degrees of specificity. Reliable, accurate, and meaningful assessment of participation performance can be achieved if an instructor bases the assessment on criteria that are known to all students, are operationally defined, and are reinforced by the instructor.

BARS — Behaviorially Anchored Rating Scales

There is an approach that can enhance objectivity and moderate subjectivity in assessments. Further, explicit performance criteria can be identified and made known to all students. When students are aware of the specific criteria, their anxiety should diminish, since there is less fear of the unknown. Because criteria are both known and operationally defined, the approach can enhance classroom involvement and discussion. As a side benefit, the approach requires student participation from the start in generating understandable performance criteria.

The approach involves the use of behaviorly anchored rating scales, or BARS. The fundamental research by Smith and Kendall (1963) guides the development and use of the scales. For the past several years, I have experimented with and used such scales in several performance contexts, including the assessment of student participation.Behaviorally anchored rating scales were designed (Smith and Kendall, 1963) as a performance assessment tool. Typically, they are a set of scales corresponding to each of the major dimensions of a job or task. On each scale are placed a set of anchors or statements that illustrate behavior on the particular job dimension. For example, in this article the performance dimension is participation in class discussion. One can identify participation in class discussion as the "job" and construct two or more scales to address quality, quantity, and other dimensions.

A series of statements is used to form a scale against which performance may be assessed. The development of these statements or anchors requires some use of class time at the beginning of the course, and this scale construction requires several steps. BARS are not typically generalized from course to course. That is, if one wishes to use scales to assess performance, it may be necessary to repeat the development process with each class or group of students.

How BARS Are Developed

Following is the step-by-step process by which the scales are developed:

1. Explain to the students that participation is an important component of the course and of their grade. Also, a useful guide is to be constructed that will help them in their performance in the course.

2. Give each of the students 3x5 cards and ask them to write at least one example (preferably two or three) of each of the following:

- Poor performance in class discussion

- Adequate performance in class discussion

- Good performance in class discussion

- Collect the cards and tell the students that the second round of the activity will occur at the next scheduled class meeting. Go about your planned activities for the remainder of the class session.

3. Have a panel of colleagues (two or three), graduate assistants, or honors students review the responses listed on the cards. Ambiguous responses, duplicate responses, and non-behavioral episodes must be removed. The panel members then rewrite the remaining items into the "expectations" format, e.g., "The student could be expected to _____. " These statements are then typed as a list of statements. My experience indicates that a class of 15 to 30 students will have generated a usable list of performance behaviors in the range of from 22 to 28 statements.

4. Give the list to the students at the next scheduled class meeting. Ask them to rank all statements (items) using 1 to rank the lowest level and 7 to rank the highest level of performance. Tell them to carefully consider each item and to make distinctions regarding level of performance by using roughly equivalent quantities of 1's, 2's, and so on in their rankings. Students seem to take this activity seriously.

5. At this point, each of the statements (items) has a set of rankings or "scores." These rankings for each statement are to be averaged. For each statement the standard deviation of the rankings must also be calculated. Typically, the statements that have standard deviations of less than 1.5 (for a 7-point scale) can be used to construct the scale.

6. Prepare the final scale. (See Figure 1 for the format and general appearance.) Place the statement you want to use on the scale at the point approximating the average value of the statement. At least six items must anchor the scale. You may have a pool of items that meet the standard deviation criterion, in which case you have some latitude in choice of statements to anchor the scale.

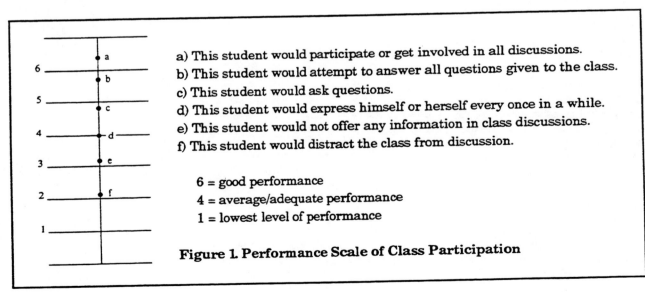

a) This student would participate or get involved in all discussions.
b) This student would attempt to answer all questions given to the class.
c) This student would ask questions.
d) This student would express himself or herself every once in a while.
e) This student would not offer any information in class discussions.
f) This student would distract the class from discussion.

6 = good performance
4 = average/adequate performance
1 = lowest level of performance

Figure 1. Performance Scale of Class Participation

7. Duplicate the scale, distribute it to the students, and discuss what it means and how it is to be used. For example, have copies of the scale produced and every three or four weeks during the semester give each student a copy of the scale with your written comments regarding behavior observed in relation to scale anchors. You might tell students how they need to improve, and/or you can reinforce positive behavior.

Developing the scale is itself a learning experience because it requires students to face the question of what constitutes good or poor performance (Bushardt, Fowler, and Debnath, 1985). The scale yields anchors or statements that should have similar meanings for all participants — students and the instructor. The performance review of any given student should be superior to most other methods of assessment because of the performance-related feedback possible with BARS. Areas in which the student can show improvement can be identified.

Student participation in the development of the appraisal instrument should result in greater student acceptance of the evaluations tendered by the instructor. A number of grading options exists for the instructor in the use of scales such as these. The specific grading features should be announced at the session when the completed scale is presented to the class.

Summary and Conclusions

What has been demonstrated has been a short-cut method of the application of the BARS approach (Green et al., 1981). The approach can be creatively applied in a variety of instructional settings. The potential benefits are many, as student motivation is improved as a result of clearer performance expectations. The domain of performance is explained in terms of acceptable and unacceptable behaviors. Subjectivity about expectations and assessments can be moderated. If expectations are made known and if they are operationally defined, we can expect student anxiety in classroom situations to be diminished. Although not the final answer, the BARS methodology can help students and faculty achieve classroom objectives.

References

Armstrong, M., & Boud, D. "Assessing Participation in Discussion: An Exploration of the Issues." *Studies in Higher Education*, 8 (1983): 33-44.

Bushardt, S.C.; Fowler, A.R, Jr.; & Debnath, S.C. "Behaviorally Anchored Rating Scales: A Valuable Aid to the Personnel Function." *Akron Business and Economic Review*, Summer 1985: 26-32.

Clarke, E.G. "Grading Seminar Performance." *College Teaching*, 33 (1985) : 129-133.

Fisher, D. "An Approach to Evaluating Class Participation." *Educational Horizons*, 53 (1975): 161-163.

Green, S.B.; Sauser, W.I., Jr.; Fagg, J.N.; & Champion, L.C.H. "Shortcut Methods for Deriving Behaviorally Anchored Rating Scales." *Educational and Psychological Measurement*, 41 (1981): 761-775.

Greive, D., ed. *Teaching In College*. Cleveland, OH: Info-Tec, Inc., 1983.

Smith, P.C., & Kendall, L.M. "Retranslation of Expectations: An Approach to the Construction of Unambiguous Anchors for Rating Scales." *Journal of Applied Psychology*, 47 (1963): 149-155.

Wood, A.E. "Experiences with Small Group Tutorials." *Studies in Higher Education*, 4 (1979): 203-209.

Grading Seminar Performance

Edward G. Clarke

Next to texts and lectures, classroom discussions and seminars are the most common approaches to teaching in American higher education (Kozma et al., 1978). Seminars commonly mean a small number of advanced students whose research is presented and critically reviewed by class and instructor. More generally, however, discussion techniques can be used in any course when students are encouraged to develop personal insights in an atmosphere of reflective thinking or problem solving (Hoover, 1980). Success in seminar and discussion calls upon a wide range of verbal skills such as speaking, listening and formulating, and responding to questions. This paper will propose an approach to evaluating these skills which is suitable to both seminars and classroom discussions.

Seminar courses are offered by virtually every college and university across the country, and research indicates that structured classroom discussions are increasingly popular with faculty members (Hoover, 1980; Armstrong and Boud, 1983; Wood, 1979) and students (Eash and Bennet, 1964). Why is this the case?

This surge is partially the result of an effort over the past ten years to clarify the goals and outcomes of a college education (McKeachie, 1978). On such lists are found cognitive skills and personal qualities which are not readily stimulated either by the passive participation encouraged in the lecture hall or the solitary scholarship of the textbook. Increasingly, college educators are turning to student-centered techniques, such as discussion and seminars.

Research on the use of these approaches indicates that college teachers are correct in their hopes for the potential of seminars and class discussion (Barnes, 1979; Smith, 1978). While it is clear that bodies of knowledge cannot be transmitted efficiently through discussion, there is nonetheless a wide and important spectrum of outcomes for both students and faculty which this technique can promote.

For the student there are both personal and skill goals (Kozma et al., 1978; McKeachie, 1978). Personally, discussion techniques can affect attitude change, increase sensitivity and motivation, explore questions of values and encourage responsibility. Discussion also can promote higher cognitive skills (integration, synthesis and creativity), problem solving, critical thinking and communication (listening, questioning, etc.). The teacher also has goals consistent with a classroom discussion approach, such as fostering faculty-student relationships, developing a less authoritative teaching style, and promoting peer learning and the study of nonstandard or interdisciplinary materials (Kuzirian, 1980; Smith, 1978).

This paper will:

- examine common problems encountered in using classroom discussion, particularly in seminars;

- describe a seminar format used at Wadhams Hall Seminary-College that avoided most of the common pitfalls of these techniques; and

- examine the use of these techniques in other institutional settings.

Problems of a Seminar Discussion Approach

Difficulties with the use of this approach can be divided into two principal areas, namely problems with conducting discussions and seminars, and problems in evaluating them.

Some problems in conducting these classes are student-centered (Andrews and Dietz, 1982). There is often a feeling that one really cannot prepare for a discussion since one never knows what will arise in the give and take of the conversation. Some students will not be motivated to discuss topics which they find dull or beyond their grasp. Many students are not able to participate effectively since they enter college without the required skills of listening, speaking clearly and persuasively, etc.

Other problems are clearly more faculty-centered. Many instructors tend to dominate discussions with authoritative behavior (McKnight, 1978). Many are unaware of how to run an effective discussion (Journet and Journet, 1979). Most importantly, few faculty members reflect on why they want the students to discuss a topic (Hoover, 1980).

A final set of problems related to conducting discussions is rooted in the environment. For example, certain aspects of the classroom situation, such as the arrangement of chairs, can inhibit effective discussion (Kuzirian, 1980).

The second major category of difficulties arises in evaluating seminar and discussion performance. Some instructors believe that evaluation is impossible, due to the highly subjective nature of such assessments (Armstrong and Boud, 1983). Others believe that evaluation of oral contributions is undesirable since grading tends to increase student anxiety and thus to inhibit the discussion (Haines and McKeachie, 1967). Some authors assert that evaluation should focus on discussion skills exhibited during the conversations. Such process skills as listening and questioning are usually evaluated only quantitatively using charts which tally the number of instances of the desired behavior (Hoover, 1980; Westcott, 1982; Hansen, 1983; Fisher, 1975; Pendergrass and Wood, 1976). Finally, some believe that qualitative evaluation of the content of discussions cannot avoid excessive subjectivity. Further, faculty members monitoring subtle qualitative variables may experience difficulty in fully participating in the class and/or modelling the desired behavior.

Fortunately, a growing body of research (Armstrong and Boud, 1983) indicates that objective assessment of classroom performance is both possible and desirable. With these difficulties — conducting and evaluating — in mind, the following course design was created and tested.

A Successful Seminar Format

This format has been in use at Wadhams Hall Seminary-College for seven years in a variety of courses, such as interdisciplinary seminars on Science and Religion and Contemporary Moral Problems, and in conjunction with the "Cosmos" television series by Carl Sagan. Normally speaking, these courses enroll approximately 10 upperclassmen and are often team-taught. Classes meet once a week for two and one-half hours, usually at night, in a seminar room filled with lounge chairs. The courses are typically three-credit electives.

Students are informed at the outset that class participation is an important part of their grade (up to 50%) and that it will be evaluated each week. The goals for this participation are discussed in detail during the first class session and also at the midterm marking period. It is also pointed out that these same criteria will be used to evaluate any written work which may be required. These goals, developed over the years, are as follows:

1. **Content Mastery:** The student must evidence an understanding of the facts, concepts, and theories presented in the assigned readings. This ability is the basis for all higher-level skills and must be made evident by classroom comments and/or responses to questions.

2. **Communication Skills:** The student must be able to inform others in an intelligent manner what he or she knows. Ideas must be communicated clearly and persuasively. Communication skills include listening to others and understanding what they have said, responding appropriately, asking questions in a clear manner, avoiding rambling discourses or class domination, using proper vocabulary pertinent to the discussion, building on the ideas of others, etc.

3. **Synthesis/Integration:** Students must illuminate the connections between the material under consideration and other bodies of knowledge. For example, one could take several ideas from the readings or class discussions and combine them to produce a new perspective on an issue, or one could take outside materials (other classes, personal experiences, etc.) and combine them to create novel insights. Students who probe the interdisciplinary roots of the theories presented or who are able to view the author or the material from several viewpoints demonstrate this skill.

4. **Creativity:** Students must demonstrate that they have mastered the basic material and have gone on to produce their own insights. A simple repetition of ideas from the text will not suffice, nor will simply commenting on what others have said. Students must go beyond the obvious by bringing their own beliefs and imagination to bear. Creativity may be displayed by showing further implications of the material, by applying it to a new field, by finding new ways of articulating or setting the materials which produce significant insights, etc.

5. **Valuing:** The student should be able to identify the values inherent in the material studied. The underlying assumptions of the author should be identified. Furthermore, students should be able to articulate their own positions by reference to basic underlying values. The student must not simply feel something is wrong or incorrect; he or she must be able to state why, based on some hierarchy of values. In either accepting or rejecting a position, the operative values must become explicit.

This approach can now be analyzed under the previously developed problem areas of students, faculty, environment, and evaluation.

Student Aspects

Student preparation for the course is encouraged by a written assignment before each class. Twenty-four hours before class, students submit a paragraph outlining a question or area for discussion. This assignment is not graded, but it serves several useful purposes:

- It forces the students to complete their readings well before the class, thus encouraging a more leisurely and reflective class preparation.

- It allows the faculty to preview student insights, confusions, and omissions before class and thus facilitates faculty preparation.

- It ensures that every student has prepared something to say.

Some questions will be simply informational: "What does the author mean by this passage?" These students can be encouraged to move to a higher cognitive level, and thus to prepare more effectively the particular skills that the faculty seeks to encourage. Often, simply asking a student if the passage in question reminds her of anything from another class can encourage an integrative approach to the subject. Another assignment requires the student to state reasons for agreeing or disagreeing with the opinions expressed in the reading. This forces students to identify values implicit in the author's viewpoint and to contrast them with their own.

The students are clearly informed that the responsibility for moving the discussion rests with them, and that they should prepare suitably. This point is clear in the registration description for the course and is outlined in the first class. Faculty do not lecture, and long silences may occur if students are unprepared, but after the first few weeks students become equal to the challenge.

A further technique for promoting student responsibility is the "mid-course correction." In the fifth class session, time is devoted to a discussion of the progress of the class. Student suggestions are sought, and as many as possible are implemented. Typically, students accept the goals of the class but desire some change in the practicalities, such as length of reading assignments. If the faculty meet these student requests, it is as if a contract has been made between teacher and student. Complaints are reduced, and student responsibility increases.

Adequate preparation is also promoted by reading assignments. Students are informed before registration that there will be a 75-page/week reading assignment. These assignments include text materials read by all students, and outside readings drawn from the interdisciplinary areas represented. If a student is taking the course for history credit, for example, then he will be assigned outside readings predominantly in history. Since not all students have the same outside readings each week, they are encouraged to see themselves as resource persons to the class in a particular area. Such tailoring of assignments also increases student interest in the content of the course.

Students are graded every week, not only on *what* they say, but *how* they say it, as a way of strengthening communication skills. In the first few weeks these concerns tend to predominate the assessment. The weekly grading emphasizes to the students the serious nature of this concern, and the written evaluative comments which the students receive from the instructor(s) specify particular behaviors which need improvement. If certain problems persist, individual conferences are used to give precise instruction and advice concerning the point in question. Indeed, some of our best teaching occurs in such personal conferences occasioned by a D or an F grade on the previous week's performance. In contrast, the practice of issuing grades for class participation at the end of the semester holds no hope for improving the skills of the students. Frequent grading can help students identify problem areas and begin efforts to improve.

Faculty Aspects

It is clear that faculty roles are transformed in the move from the lecture hall to the seminar room. We become less a *source of information* and more a *guide to achievement*. In seminars and discussions, leadership is substituted for authority (Hoover, 1980). Further, the specification of discussion goals serves to clarify what behaviors the faculty need to model. We cannot demand that students perform creatively, for example, if they do not see creative faculty members. Our experience and the literature on college teaching indicate that certain behaviors are most important for the faculty (Hansen, 1983; Journet and Journet, 1979; Kuzirian, 1980; McKeachie, 1978; Smith 1978):

- To set goals and to evaluate behavior based on them;

- To provide background information, reading lists, etc.;

- To encourage, to stimulate, to motivate;

- To clarify, to mediate, to uphold professional standards;

- To summarize.

Further, instructors must develop questioning skills which promote discussion and do not terminate inquiry. Such a simple technique as redirecting a question to another student can usually produce the information or insight requested (satisfying the inquirer) while at the same time allowing evaluation of the second student's response.

Faculty preparation for the seminar is enhanced in several ways. The writing assignments indicate what topics will be covered by students and what areas need to be introduced by the faculty. The goals of synthesis, creativity, and valuing are the most difficult for the students to meet. Faculty preparation centers not on content but on these higher level outcomes.

The problems from failing to consider the reason for discussion techniques are ameliorated by our specifying the previously listed five major outcomes. Although presented as student goals, they clearly are originally the goals of the faculty who designed the course and serve to guide their preparation for each class.

Environmental Aspects

Our classes are held in a seminar room with lounge chairs arranged in a circle. This setting allows students to see and hear each other in a natural fashion. The course is held in the evenings for a period long enough to probe the issues in depth, allowing everyone to speak at each meeting. A relaxed atmosphere can help alleviate the anxiety which students have as they are asked to become more active through discussion.

Evaluation

Each class is tape-recorded, and evaluation normally takes place the next day. Our experience has been that two hours are normally sufficient to listen to the tape and to write comments for each student concerning his or her performance. This technique has several advantages. It allows the faculty member to participate in the discussion and not to be distracted by in-class grading. It permits more extensive remarks based on the verbatim contributions of the students. Faculty remarks are keyed to the goals; for example, a common request is for more detailed development of ideas. In extreme cases, we have met with students before class to discuss their understanding of the material and to "prepare" the comments for the evening. It has been our experience that most students actually have creative, personal insights into the material but they do not know how to cultivate these ideas. This is a skill that can be learned and faculty can teach it through discussion and careful evaluation of student performance.

The tape-recordings of class discussions often are played for students to point out particularly troublesome behavior, and they can serve as an objective record in case a dispute arises over grades at the end of the semester. (Our experience has shown, however, that such disputes are normally resolved early in the semester, after one or two weeks of unsatisfactory grades.) The tapes also permit several persons to grade the student's work if the class is team-taught.

An alternate technique has each faculty member, in turn, grade during the class period. However, this does prevent that instructor from being a resource to the discussion. The tape has the added advantage of allowing the faculty members to evaluate their own class contributions, thus encouraging faculty development related to the class goals. This technique has been particularly useful in encouraging faculty to limit the length of their contributions in order to maximize student participation.

Applications and Conclusions

It seems clear that the five goals specified at Wadhams Hall Seminary-College are not limited to discussion and seminar courses. On the contrary, they appear to be outcomes which are expressive of the entire liberal arts experience. Further, they need not be limited to oral performance; creativity, valuing, and the others are desirable outcomes for written work as well. As a result, future work in this area will examine the applicability of these techniques to evaluating oral comprehensive examinations, senior projects and other forms of written work such as term papers and essay exams.

The qualitative evaluation of seminars and classroom discussions seems to be a technique particularly suited to the current educational climate. There are two important trends active in American higher education, one proceeding from within, and one from without. Internally, colleges across the nation are returning to an emphasis on the liberal arts and a strengthening of general education and core programs (Gaff, 1983). Externally, funding agencies and accrediting groups are encouraging or insisting on better management and evaluation of educational programs. The approach outlined above permits the use of one of the oldest tools of the liberal arts — the seminar — while assuring that it is evaluated objectively. Such a strategy also has a high probability of success since it requires no new equipment or facilities (computers or otherwise), or extensive retraining. Indeed, its strength appears to be its simplicity.

References

Andrews, J.D.W., & Dietz, D. "The Self-Steering Seminar." *Journal of Higher Education*, 53 (1982): 552-567.

Armstrong, M. "Assessing Students' Participation in Class Discussion." *Assessment in Higher Education*, 3 (1978): 186-202.

Armstrong, M., & Boud, D. "Assessing Participation in Discussion: An Exploration of the Issues." *Studies in Higher Education*, 8 (1983): 33-44.

Barnes, P.W. "Leading Discussions." In Milton, Ohmer, ed., *On College Teaching*. San Francisco: Jossey-Bass, 1979. Pp. 62-100.

Carnegie Foundation for the Advancement of Teaching. *Missions of the College Curriculum*. San Francisco: Jossey-Bass, 1977.

Eash, M.J., & Bennet, E.M. "The Effect of Class Size on Achievement and Attitudes." *American Educational Research Journal*, 1 (1964): 229-239.

Fisher, D. "An Approach to Evaluating Class Participation." *Educational Horizons*, 53 (1975): 161-163.

Gaff, J. *General Education Today*. San Francisco: Jossey-Bass, 1983.

Haines, D.B., & McKeachie, W.J. "Cooperative Versus Competitive Discussion Methods of Teaching Introductory Psychology." *Journal of Educational Psychology*, 58 (1967): 386-390.

Hansen, W.L. "Improving Classroom Discussion in Economics Courses." *The Journal of Economic Education*, 14 (1983): 40-49.

Hoover, K. *College Teaching Today: A Handbook for Postsecondary Instruction*. Boston: Allyn and Bacon, 1980.

Journet, A.R.P., & Journet, D. "Structured Discussion in Introductory Biology." *Improving College and University Teaching*, 27 (1979): 167-170.

Kozma, R.; Belle, L.; & Williams, G. *Instructional Techniques in Higher Education*. Englewood Cliffs: Educational Technology Publications, 1978.

Kuzirian, E.E. " 'Everyman His Own Historian': Socratic Inquiry for Teaching European History." *Improving College and University Teaching*, 28 (1980): 124-126.

McKeachie, W.J. *Teaching Tips: A Guidebook for the Beginning College Teacher*. 7th ed. Lexington, MA: D.C. Heath, 1978.

McKnight, P.C. *On Guiding (Not Leading) Discussions*. Manhattan, KS: Center for Faculty Evaluation and Development in Higher Education, 1978.

Pendergrass, R., & Wood, D. "Facilitating Discussions: Skills for Teachers and Students." *The Clearing House*, 49 (1976): 267-270.

Smith, I.K. "Teaching with Discussions: A Review." *Educational Technology*, 18 (1978): 40-43.

Westcott, G. "Teaching and Evaluating Discussion Skills." *English Journal*, 71 (1982): 76-78.

Wood, A.E. "Experiences with Small Group Tutorials." *Studies in Higher Education*, 4 (1979): 203-209.

What to Do When Somebody Criticizes Your Teaching

Maryellen Weimer

Perhaps the best way to start is by establishing what you should *not* do — which tends to be exactly how most faculty respond to criticism about their teaching. *Don't get defensive.* That's easy advice to offer; understandably, it isn't easy to follow. Teaching requires just too much personal involvement to afford one the luxury of automatic, objective appraisal. The instructional strategies, techniques, and policies selected and implemented in a course and classroom convey important messages about the person who uses them. When a colleague suggests you're "disorganized" or a student accuses you of teaching a "boring" course, these messages say as much about *you* as about your *teaching*.

But the urge to respond defensively derives from more than the need to protect the self. Part of the urge results from the comments themselves. They are *judgmental* — sometimes excessively so. All of us, when we talk about teaching, tend to be evaluative in this way — as if an individual teacher or particular teaching technique was right or wrong, good or bad, in some absolute sense. *Nothing could be further from the truth.* Teachers and their techniques vary in their effects on individuals and vary depending on the course and even on their context within a given course.

So, it's not just that teachers are vulnerable, it's that the messages hit that vulnerability head-on. Recognize the inclination to respond defensively, but *don't do it* — at least not initially. Rather, acknowledge your vulnerability and then work to put the judgment into perspective. Try this mental procedure. Consider first the extent to which the criticism is representative. How many observers said it, out of how many who evaluated your teaching?

Often evaluations are phrased so that it sounds as if the evaluator speaks for the rest of the world. Unfair! A single observer speaks with absolute authority for only one person — herself. As much as that person might like to summon the support of others, unless others have been specifically asked, their support cannot be claimed and should not be implied. When the colleague says, "Paul, you're disorganized," what the colleague should say is, "Paul, *I* thought you were disorganized."

And it's not just that colleagues and other observers, including students, are inclined to speak for more than just themselves; they also tend to offer conclusions far more comprehensive than their observation warrants. Frequently colleagues, fulfilling requirements of well-intentioned peer-review programs, stage commando raids on classes. They drop in unannounced, never inquire what came before and what will come after, leave without ever revealing what "grading" standard they used, and then announce with authority, "Oh, she's having trouble in the classroom." Unfair! Maybe you were having trouble that day, but to conclude that every day in class is like that day assumes teachers and teaching machines have a lot in common.

On the other hand, putting judgments into perspective does not imply automatically dismissing any negative input. The perspective I'm advocating attempts to prevent the excessive amounts of defensive "noise" that make it impossible to hear sensibly what the objection might be.

For most of us, there is much we could learn about teaching effectively. And most of us could learn that from our colleagues and students, but we must be prepared to help them help us understand their criticisms.

For example, most descriptions of teaching (effective or ineffective) tend to be abstract and non-specific. So, you're "disorganized" or "boring." What does that mean? Until you know what specific behaviors, techniques, policies, or activities convey that, the information is not particularly valuable.

Press the evaluator. "You say I'm disorganized. Can you tell me some specific things I did when you saw me teach that suggested I'm disorganized?" The urge to defend may surface again. Resist it. Granted, you may never have intended what you did to suggest disorganization, and granted, the evaluator may be all wrong to think that, but the fact is that one observer decided that your use of stories "disorganized" the lecture. If you don't agree, ask others about the effects those behaviors had on them.

Talking about *behaviors* has great value because *you can do something about behaviors*. If you interject stories and illustrations that lead you off the main track and confuse students, you can fix that. One instructor we know who does this announces to the class, "I'm going off on a tangent," and moves over to the side of the room. Moreover, you can (and should) press the observer to suggest alternatives. "Well, if that confused you, what could I have done that would have made it clearer?"

Now the criticism starts to have value. You acquire from the evaluator ideas as to alternatives. Try them, if they have merit, and see what happens.

Most instructors take pride and interest in their performance in the classroom. Input from others — even a critical assessment that's well-presented — has the potential to improve that performance, but it must be unpackaged carefully and put into a proper perspective. Otherwise, the instructor just gets angry.

Five Steps to Better Teaching

Maryellen Weimer

Let's assume you're interested in teaching better — not because you're doing badly and therefore, by your (or somebody else's) assessment, "need" to teach better — but because you care and you'd like to try. Many of us we try, regularly, to teach more effectively. When we fail, it's not for lack of trying, but perhaps we aren't as successful as we might be because our approach is *reactionary*.

We get some student evaluations indicating they don't find feedback on their assignments useful, so we try to fix that. Or two students nail us after class about the homework problems, so we do something about them. Or we hear from a colleague about a good idea on pop quizzes, so we decide to try that. An approach like this essentially hit-and-miss. We lack some sort of process or framework or context in which to orient our activities.

Consider this five-step process as a more *systematic* way to teach better, a framework that gives individual activities greater coherence. Using it, we'll be making decisions in some sort of context, which should result in more reasoned and informed choices.

Step 1: **Develop Instructional Awareness.**

Begin with honest, soul-searching self-assessment. If you find yourself stuck on the issue of whether or not you're a good or bad teacher, you're already off on the wrong track. Rather, search to discover *how* you teach. Watch what you do in class. Write a one-page description of your style that would enable someone to pick you out of a group of teachers. Look at those strategies and techniques and ask yourself if inherent in them aren't some interesting assumptions. What does the way you teach say about how you think people learn? In other words, begin by enlarging, clarifying, possibly even rectifying your understanding of how you teach. Premise: You can't possibly make reasoned choices about what you could do and should do if you don't have clear understanding of what you do.

Step 2: **Seek Input.**

Teaching requires a great deal of self-investment, which makes objectivity difficult. In other words, what you decide about how you teach in Step One needs to be measured against insights others may offer about your teaching. Seek input from colleagues and students in three different arenas; ask them to describe how you teach, ask them to describe how what you do affects them, and ask them to suggest other, possibly more effective ways of doing what you do. Note here the continuing and deliberate effort to avoid putting these activities in a judgmental context. That makes it all the harder for you to be objective, and much of what we do and believe about teaching is not clearly or absolutely right or wrong, good or bad. The effects of teaching behaviors, policies and practices, like most everything else in the world, vary a great deal.

Step 3: **Make Choices.**

Make choices about what ought to be changed and make choices about how to change it. The key is using the information acquired in the Steps One and Two to inform those choices. If you know how you teach, what you believe about teaching, about students and learning, you have a much better sense of what you can honestly and effectively do in the classroom. If you use essay exams, you probably use them because you believe they most effectively teach the thinking skills you see as a top educational priority. If students object, if colleagues object, weigh that input against why you do what you do. You may legitimately decide not to change. But you might consider the possibility of changing the surrounding activities, such as how you prepare students for the exams or how you offer feedback, without changing the practice itself. On the other hand, not all we do in the classroom reflects our priorities. Some practices may even contradict them. You can change those practices much more readily, much more dramatically, and with less soul-searching.

How should you change what you do? Again, knowing how you teach and collecting ideas as to alternatives facilitates this part of the process. Lots of ideas may have appeal, but they may not fit with the content and objectives of the course. Of course, you can't run a large introductory class as you'd run a senior seminar. Different presentational ideas, tactics, and strategies abound, but will they fit comfortably with your teaching style?

Step 4: **Implement the Alterations.**

Do it systematically and incrementally. In other words, give the change a fair chance. Don't do it halfheartedly or with skimpy preparation. This fair chance also implies making what you change the object of your fixed and focused attention. You can't do that if you're implementing eight changes the same day or in the same course. The most effective improvement of instruction is ongoing and gradual. Behavior changes especially take time to incorporate. Old habits sometimes die hard. You can't change how you teach without doing some work. Given the time pressures that face us all, improvement becomes a much more manageable proposition if we commit to it regularly but in reasonable chunks. Work on your exams next semester, your questioning strategies after that, your feedback mechanisms after that, and so on — probably until you retire.

Step 5: **Seek Input About the Alterations.**

This step brings you back, full circle. You first seek input from yourself. What are you doing now? How is it working? What are the implications of these new policies and practices? Are they consistent with what you know and believe about yourself as a teacher? Seek input second from your colleagues and students. How do they respond to the change? Do they have alterations of the alteration to suggest?

This process doesn't propose a new and revolutionary way to alter instruction, but it does offer a way of putting what tend too often to be isolated activities into a framework. It also changes the improvement process from *reactive* to *proactive*.

We begin by looking at how we teach, possibly identifying some areas where we question what we do. Input from others helps us to clarify our concerns and gives us ideas as to alternatives. Then we make choices, decisions about *what* to change and how to change it, based on an understanding of *how* and *why* we teach as we do. We look for new activities, rather than having them find us. And we implement changes in a *reasoned* and *systematic* way, subjecting them to the scrutiny of ourselves and others.